Revolutionary Syndicalism
and French Labor

By the Same Author

European Society in Upheaval (1967)
Priest and Revolutionary: Lamennais and the Dilemma of French Catholicism (1967)
Modern Europe (1969)
A Century for Debate (1969)

Revolutionary Syndicalism and French Labor:

A Cause without Rebels

By Peter N. Stearns

*HD
6684
S73*

135174

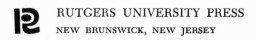

RUTGERS UNIVERSITY PRESS

NEW BRUNSWICK, NEW JERSEY

For Deborah

Contents

List of Abbreviations of Commonly Cited References

AD   Archives départementales
AN   Archives nationales
APS   Archives de la Préfecture de police de la Seine
BOT   *Bulletin de l'Office du travail*
STAT   Direction du travail, *Statistique des grèves et recours à
        conciliation, 1899–1914*. 15 vols. Paris, 1900–1915.
VP   *La Voix du peuple*.

Revolutionary Syndicalism
and French Labor

Introduction

Most historians who know anything about French labor between 1890 and and 1914 and some who know a great deal would claim that revolutionary syndicalism was its most striking attribute. In contrast with German workers, who can be described as well-organized socialists, a significant segment of French labor combined an antipolitical approach with their socialism or rejected politics altogether. Unlike pragmatic British trade unions, French unions, or at least the main union movement, stood for revolt by means of a general strike. Syndicalism,[1] the argument runs, corresponded to the revolutionary tradition of French workers and to their pervasive individualism, for it sought to attack the existing order without forming any massive alternative organization.[2]

This view is at best a good guess, for it has never been seriously tested. Historians, being to some degree intellectuals, too often look at the expressed ideas of a movement or organization without checking the extent to which the ideas were held by participants or manifested in their behavior. It is more convenient to stick to the ideological level, for this is generally preserved in writing. Labor historians usually sympathize with the cause they are studying and want to believe that workers believed in it. Ironically, though committed to history "from the bottom up" when discussing workers and society as a whole, they fail to apply this principle to labor history as soon as they can find organized movements or doctrines to study.[3]

In the case of prewar French labor, this approach has led, at the textbook level, to a summary of worker attitudes as cited by Georges Sorel. But effective syndicalism considerably antedates Sorel's writings, and Sorel was not close to the actual syndicalist union movement before

1914. We must therefore ascertain, before relying extensively on his writings, that he correctly interpreted the movement. In more detailed studies, historians have gone deeper, usually by citing resolutions of the leading national labor group, the Confédération générale du travail (C.G.T.), drawn from the annual congresses. This method, besides being frequently dull, is again inadequate, for it assumes without question that the C.G.T. was representative of its members.[4]

We need, then, a new look at the French labor movement. We need to end, or at least to examine, anomalies such as that appearing in a recent study of French strikes after 1919,[5] which notes, in the evaluation of actual agitation, how peaceful and moderate French workers were but then goes on to repeat the whole litany on the dominance of revolutionary traditions, including syndicalism, in French labor. We know amazingly little about the working classes in France at the turn of the century, indeed after the Second Empire, because historians have been so preoccupied with tracing doctrinal disputes and political machinations in parties and in unions. And if we know little about the workers, how much do we really know about the movements they participated in?

This study questions some stereotypes about French labor, such as whether or not workers, in a twenty-year period in one European country, accepted the ideology that guided many of their admitted leaders, and makes a plea for historians and indeed anyone interested in past or present society to test the impact of social ideas, to be skeptical about the persistent tendency to approach labor or any social group through formal doctrines and the pronouncements of leaders. France at the turn of the century provides a striking illustration of the importance of other avenues of inquiry, but the issue is general. Most people are not intellectuals. We know too little, even in modern history, about how ideas are disseminated and absorbed. Historians of European labor tend to assume that workers are easily motivated by ideas or that their economic motivations parallel the ideas to which they are exposed. This study offers one test case of the problem.

Syndicalism was of course an extraordinary doctrine, far more thoroughly revolutionary than Marxism. Did significant numbers of French workers want revolution? Did they at least cherish syndicalism as a myth? If not, why was syndicalism a part of the French labor movement at all? Was it an accident, a doctrine brought in from outside the working classes and partially adopted because it was there, not because it was particularly applicable? Can revolutionary rhetoric flourish if the situation is not revolutionary, or conversely can we assume that a situation is revolutionary if revolutionary rhetoric is at least tolerated by a large social group? Here is a special instance of the problem of testing formal ideas by actual beliefs and practices.

These questions about French syndicalism have to be answered if we are to develop a coherent theory of protest in industrial Europe. Much of the work on modern agitation generalizes broadly about nonindustrial as well as industrial societies.[6] From the standpoint of European history, we know more about the nature of preindustrial protest, through 1848, including the relationship between ideological movements and currents of unrest, than we do about agitation after the advent of explicitly revolutionary ideologies and the expansion of the ranks of professional agitators. By implication, statements on the nature of preindustrial protest begin to define industrial protest. A recent essay tries to make the definition clear: modern protest (which in France began to take shape in the 1850s) is political, organized, and progressive in the sense of seeking new instead of old rights.[7] Syndicalism fits this definition rather uncomfortably. It sought to organize protest but very loosely. It was political but in a curious way. It looked to positive gains and new producers' rights but it was also antimodern in its appeal to craft traditions. Perhaps, then, it was a transitional protest doctrine, in which case French workers were slower fully to modernize their protest than workers in other countries. Or were protest forms really independent of syndicalism and in greater harmony with the modern model?

The notion that syndicalism characterized much of French labor has been accepted, by Frenchmen and non-Frenchmen alike, because it seems to be typically French. Revolutionary, violent, antiorganization, individualistic—these terms seem to describe both the French character and syndicalism.[8] To view French labor in terms of "national character" is indeed appealing in many ways. But it must be tested against other national labor movements at the time to show what is distinctively French. The question goes beyond the labor movement alone, for an emphasis on syndicalism reinforces generally held notions of French inaptitude for industrial society.

An examination of French workers and syndicalism exposes one final problem, if it cannot fully resolve it. Historians must pay more attention to the actual process of workers' accommodation to industrial society, and this particularly in France. It is astonishing how seldom historians or sociologists have tried to test catchwords like "alienation" or "anomie" among workers in the past. The problem is complicated of course by the lack of agreement on what alienation consists of and whom it is most likely to affect. The Marxist focus on the alienation of workers from the process and products of their work has often been shifted to groups with higher or more diffuse aspirations, though this has mainly been applied recently and in the United States, where expectations are higher than they were in earlier industrial situations. Still, sociologists and a variety of popularizers return to the idea that the factory system produces alienation among workers, which is reflected in the concern for rewards instead of worthy performance on the job.[9] It is difficult to assess this sort of alienation among contemporary workers, since outsiders must intervene at some point to make judgments. A historical interpretation is still more remote, yet some attempts must ultimately be made. The task is greatly simplified for France when syndicalism is taken literally, for its hostility to industrial life was intense. Historians of France tend at least implicitly to assume that French workers sensed the alienation of factory life and whenever possible resisted industrial forms and methods. French industrialization surged from the mid-1890s until World War I and beyond. What was the workers' reaction and what part did syndicalism play in it?

This study depends on a knowledge of what French workers wanted apart from the pronouncements of their leaders. Many workers spoke rather directly for themselves. True, relatively few "ordinary" workers left written records about life and conditions, and French social scientists lagged in investigations of worker responses. But there are two ways of testing how syndicalism or any modern labor doctrine coincides with workers' real goals. The first is through a study of voting patterns. Theoretically, syndicalist workers should not have voted at all, and it has been argued that high rates of abstentions in areas like French Lorraine were due to syndicalist protests against the whole political order. I think it more probable that such abstentions resulted from a lack of political consciousness on the part of workers involved, who in areas like Lorraine were quite new to industry. The presence of many foreigners, particularly Italians, doubtless deterred political awareness by hampering political organization even among French workers. At the same time, many professed syndicalists did vote, mainly for socialist candidates, in an effort to press for change through political as well as economic methods. Voting patterns might, then, tell more than we now know about the extent and fervor of syndicalist convictions, but they are cumbersome to use and hard to interpret.

Far more significant are the patterns of strike activity in the period, which reveal both the tactics and the goals that workers were willing to pursue. Strikes were of course influenced by leaders and ideas, both often syndicalist, but they were seldom totally controlled by either. The spontaneous element present in most strikes reveals more about workers' conditions and attitudes than any study of formal union or syndicalist programs can. Though admittedly the commitment was episodic, strikes involved a deeper commitment to protest than did socialist voting or mere membership in a syndicalist union, since the participants sacrificed material resources and emotional energy and sometimes risked arrest, dismissal, and physical violence.

From 1899 until 1907, the strike rate increased markedly in France, as in most European countries. Between 1890 and 1900, the average annual rate of strikes in France was 421; in 1899 there were 740 strikes, and at no time before 1915 did the rate fall below 500. An average of 92,448 workers struck each year during the 1890s; between 1900–1914, the figure ranged from 90,000 in 1908 to 509,224 in 1906. This meant that the percentage of employed labor in manufacturing and transport annually participating in strikes more than doubled after 1900. From slightly under 3% in the average year in the 1890s it rose to over 7%. Despite important fluctuations, all indices of strike activity showed growing intensity during most of the prewar period. The first attempt at a nation-wide strike occurred in 1906; the first effective industry-wide strikes began with the miners' rising of 1902. During the two decades before World War I, almost every conceivable method of striking was tried, often for the first time. None of this involved more than a minority of the working class, but it was a sizeable minority. During the whole period from 1899 through 1914, strikes by industrial and transport workers involved a total of 3,304,482 participants.[10] Many workers struck several different times, of course; but it can be assumed that at least a million manufacturing workers went on strike at least once. This is the primary reason for using strikes as a test of working-class syndicalism. The strike rate showed that there was a mounting wave of working-class protest. Syndicalism was advancing at the same time. After the death in 1901 of Fernand Pelloutier, who had distrusted strikes and stressed the unions' role in educating workers, syndicalist leaders regarded themselves above all as fomenters of strikes.[11] If a study of strikes shows that, in fact, syndicalism had only limited relevance to actual protest, then its hold on workers must have been slight. Unhappily, strikes have not heretofore been intensively studied, for they are usually treated as a minor corollary of an institutional or ideological study of the union movement. This is a major cause of the superficiality of many comments on French labor and on modern working-class protest generally, which this book is intended to counteract.

My attention to the problem of determining the connection between syndicalism and ordinary workers means that the book is something less than a complete study of syndicalism. Such studies already exist, which is one reason to avoid repetition here. My own ultimate interest is in trying to ascertain how workers behaved and what they wanted, outside of as well as within protest movements; but to do this the role of labor movements such as syndicalism must be assessed. In studying the impact of syndicalism, I think I am summing up the leading elements of syndicalism as a labor movement; indeed much of this essay concerns the problems of institutionalizing as well as popularizing a radical doctrine. But again, it is not a complete history. This may bother some readers, for there seems to be a certain ritual to labor history that requires the same figures to be mentioned and the same doctrines evoked, regardless of the precise topic. The names of Sorel and other syndicalist theorists appear infrequently in these pages, because their ideas had little direct influence on workers in this period and such names were not generally known to them. The discussions of socialism by syndicalists and of syndicalism by socialists receive scant attention because they are familiar enough already and because they do not convey what syndicalism meant to most of the working class. Some readers may disagree with my choice of topic but still find value in the study as a preliminary to renewed attention to the development of syndicalist theory; for obviously the theorists discussed many of the implications of the uncomfortable relation between syndicalist doctrine and the interests of ordinary workers. My only point here is that this is not my subject: I am studying syndicalism as an active force among workers and those syndicalist leaders who were labor organizers. My source material, like my presentation, has been developed with the idea of examining syndicalism from the bottom up, not from the top down. Hence fair warning is given that many of the familiar signposts along the path of the French labor movement will be ignored.

Two final matters. This study has a quantitative aspect, as any study of a social group must have, but it relies on only partially quantifiable materials. I can safely talk of numbers of strikes and strikers, but this is not enough. I cannot say how many workers were syndicalists or were exposed to syndicalism. I cannot say how many workers struck for goals different from those listed in the official strike statistics. I must estimate, on the basis of qualitative evidence. Hence, in what follows, the reader will find more references to "some" or "many" than may please him. I apologize but I know no remedy. For the usual ploy, to refer to "the workers" or "the class," is unacceptable. It is more forceful, neater, but it is false. There were very few characteristics common to all workers. We must go beyond stereotypes about social classes and must combine impressionistic with numerical evidence to do this. We must accept some vagueness in phrasing to avoid far more misleading generalizations.

For, questions of phrasing aside, a major drawback in viewing workers through a formal labor movement is that the viewers are inclined to look for a unified or unifiable working class. At most, they might note the contrast between, say, workers who were syndicalist and those who were not. In fact, one of the real difficulties facing any labor movement in the period was that worker interests varied greatly with region, industry, and individual personality. If, in discussing some of the major divergences, I add complexity, I add reality as well. Syndicalism was a movement aimed at working-class control of economy and society; but many workers were satisfied with things as they were, others worked only for gains within the system, while others did indeed want more voice. Perhaps, in this peak period of worker agitation, there was no working class at all, but rather a motley collection of traditionalists, would-be bourgeois, and genuine proletarian radicals.

The brief bibliography at the end of the book offers suggestions for further secondary reading. Materials for this study are drawn primarily from labor and governmental sources. Accounts by labor leaders, particularly national figures who participated in major strikes, are abundant and informative in France—this was one of the fruits of the syndicalists' interest in strikes, for no other country has so rich a literature. As a vital supplement and, sometimes, a corrective to these sources, government statistics and manuscript police reports of strikes offer abundant information. The French police were also unique in their comprehensive coverage of labor agitation, so we know not only the number of strikes but also how they started and were conducted.

I can only briefly suggest the assistance received from many quarters in the preparation of the book. I am grateful to the archivists of the Archives nationales and of numerous departmental archives for their advice and aid. The kindness of officials at the archives of the Prefecture of Police, the Fédération du bâtiment, and the Fédération des typographes was deeply appreciated. Mme Denise Fauvel-Rouif, at the Institut français d'histoire sociale, helped guide me through some useful collections of pamphlet material.

The faculty research funds of the College and of the Social Sciences Division of the University of Chicago provided substantial financial support for this project. The staff of the Computational Center of the University of Chicago was exceedingly helpful in tabulating statistical information; Miss Cynthia Pemberton prepared materials for the computer with intelligence and accuracy. Nancy Stearns assisted my research in France and provided vital wifely encouragement. She and Mrs. Marilyn Jacobsen typed the manuscript; Professor John Wilson gathered some of the statistical material. Professor Carter Jefferson was kind enough to read the manuscript and offer several useful suggestions. I must particularly thank my research assistant, Gerald Oppenheimer, for carrying through some demanding phases of these investigations.

1 Syndicalism: Its Development and Symptoms

Origins and Ideology

Syndicalism was never a very clearly defined doctrine. It stressed three key points: complete hostility to the existing system; a belief that the only way to attack this system was by economic rather than political means, notably a great general strike; and a vague indication that the future society would be organized without a central political structure, on the basis of local economic units directed by producers themselves. The haziness about the nature of the ultimate goals was common to many revolutionary doctrines of course, including Marxism.

Syndicalist hostility to capitalist society was just as vigorous as Marxist hostility, though it lacked elaborate historical or economic arguments as a buttress. In the syndicalist view, capitalism meant exploitation of man by man, fat profits for a few drawn from the sweat of the many. Capitalism tainted everything. The state, in particular, was nothing more than a tool of capitalist dominion. All this had to be swept away; the need for revolution was unquestionable. But the revolutionary tactic had to be new; the old idea of capturing the state was no longer valid. Hence the stress on a general strike, which would paralyze the economy and bring down the state.

This concept, one of the hallmarks of syndicalism, clearly distinguishing it from Marxism, resulted from several considerations. The weapons the state possessed, with its big armies and police forces, doomed any frontal attack to failure. The lessons of the Paris Commune, which influenced syndicalist thinking strongly, showed that even a vigorous political confrontation could be suppressed by force. The general strike would circumvent the state, because the latter would find no precise target for suppression and would be overwhelmed by the sheer number of people involved. Syndicalists admitted that violence would probably be necessary in the strike, but they believed that their tactic was realistic, indeed that any other approach was impractical or not genuinely revolutionary. But the emphasis on economic weapons was not simply pragmatic. Syndicalists had a profound distrust of politics. Obviously capitalist politics was dirty, and syndicalists felt that any contact with it, even an effort to use it for revolutionary purposes, would sully the purity of a revolutionary movement without advancing its purposes. And since there was to be no formal state in the future, there was no need to work to control it in the present; the state should simply be undermined. This was the most important source of disagreement between syndicalists and Marxists.

Syndicalism sought to end economic injustice, to eliminate radical inequalities in earnings, and to turn over to the actual producers the fruits of their labors. Characteristically, however, formulas about future distribution of income were not spelled out clearly. For the syndicalist aim, far more single-mindedly than the Marxist, despite important goals in common, was for individual freedom. The idea of a localized society, run by producers' units under direct, democratic control, was designed to give each individual maximum liberty and subject him to no decisions in which he had not participated. Syndicalists hated and feared the constraints of organization. No massive organizations were permitted either in the future society or in the attack on the present order. Economic injustice would naturally crumble when the real producers could make decisions for themselves.

Syndicalism, like any good protest doctrine, offered a variety of attractions. For someone consumed with hatred for the present, without great concern for what would come next or even how it would come, syndicalism had real appeal. Doubtless the majority of the participants in syndicalist movements, perhaps even a majority of the leaders, were particularly drawn by the immediacy and apparent feasibility of the general strike; syndicalist tactics seemed more unambiguously revolutionary than those of any other movement in the decade or two before World War I.[1] And for people disturbed about the basic direction of society, syndicalism offered not just a tactic but a reasonably clear and complete alternative.

Part of the vagueness and apparent simplicity of the syndicalist approach resulted from the origins of the movement, or rather the lack of precise origins. No single thinker or organizer presided over the birth of the movement. Syndicalism can be seen as the natural product of the traditions of French labor, emerging gradually in the second half of the nineteenth century, which is one reason that an assessment of its importance is so essential. The most significant intellectual forerunner of syndicalism was Pierre-Joseph Proudhon, the artisan who made France's greatest contribution to socialist thought and was one of the few non-Marxist socialists of any importance after 1848. Proudhon's thinking dominated French labor movements in the third quarter of the nineteenth century and syndicalism was in many ways the logical successor. But Proudhon's thinking had spelled out only the goals that syndicalism took up, not the methods. For these we must turn in part to even older French traditions of protest. From the Revolution of 1789 on, some agitators had urged revolution for its own sake, without great concern for what would come next. Adolphe Blanqui was the leading advocate of this approach during much of the nineteenth century; from the Blanquist tradition came many syndicalist leaders, notably Victor Griffuelhes, the head of the C.G.T. during the early twentieth century. Obviously the promotion of a general strike was a new twist, but its immediacy and revolutionary aim made syndicalism heir to the tradition of glorification of revolution that had its roots in certain aspects of Jacobinism. Finally, about 1900, syndicalism benefited from an influx of revolutionary anarchist leaders, who saw in syndicalism a more realistic and slightly better organized means of destroying the existing order and who could revel in the freedom from constraint that the movement promised both before and after the revolution.

The intellectual underpinnings of syndicalism meant that the movement stemmed from and had particular appeal for a number of key groups. The groups can be defined in different and somewhat overlapping ways. Syndicalism attracted many workers raised in a trade-union tradition. Trade unions antedated a political labor movement in France, notably under the Second Empire. It is more common for workers to begin their expression of grievance with a union movement, which is easier to organize than political action; and the government of the Second Empire facilitated the formation of unions while discouraging labor politics. Union traditions in this early period were strengthened by Proudhonism, which distrusted political methods; this gave an ideology to trade-unionist resistance to politics, to the desire to rely on direct efforts within the economy that developed without the ideology in many countries, including England and the United States. Part of syndicalism, then, was a doctrinal trade-unionism. The syndicalist approach also had special appeal to craftsmen. Artisans like printers and carpenters had the longest trade-union traditions in France as in most countries. Some of them also had a traditional if intermittent contact with the French revolutionary impulse; the professions most open to syndicalism, notably the building trades, were, on the whole, the same as those that had provided the bulk of the men who manned the barricades in 1830 and 1848. The syndicalist stress on local organization and producers' control of their own work appealed to even older artisanal traditions; vaguely and in obviously radical language, syndicalism seemed to suggest something like a restoration of idealized guilds. Emphasis on small size and participant control of economic organization in the interests of economic justice and equality certainly recalled the guild tradition; Proudhon's thought had intellectualized this artisanal heritage. Finally syndicalism had particular appeal to workers in Paris, partly because of the city's unusually intense revolutionary tradition, which included, in the glorification of the Commune, hostility to the whole apparatus of central government and vigorous attachment to the Jacobin notion of direct democracy. Syndicalism sprang from trade-unionists, artisans, and Parisians. These sources gave the movement real strength. But how completely were they won over to it? And how far did syndicalism spread among other types of workers and outside Paris?

Syndicalism began to emerge in the 1880s. French labor movements of all sorts had ground to a halt in the 1870s, because of the defeat of the Commune in 1871 and subsequent repression. The trade unions that existed before the 1884 law that granted legal freedom to the formation of unions were mainly local, isolated, and rather conservative. Then, with the possibilities that the 1884 law afforded, the first important associations of unions arose on a local basis. That is, unions from various professions, like printing and baking, grouped in a city-wide federation, a *bourse du travail;* national federations in the same profession followed more slowly. The *bourse du travail* movement, which federated very loosely at the national level in the 1890s, both reflected and furthered a syndicalist tendency. The movement avoided politics (as did many early unions, which had to draw workers of various political persuasions). More than this, it soon turned against politics—somewhat ironically, since most of the local *bourses* served as employment offices (labor exchanges) and as such received government funds. Moreover, the localist stress of the movement and its largely artisanal composition (industrial groups like miners and textile workers seldom played a major role) furthered syndicalism. The head of the *bourse du travail* movement, Fernand Pelloutier, was the first real articulator of syndicalist ideas. In the late 1890s, the Fédération des bourses du travail set up a general strike committee (even earlier, in the late 1880s, general labor congresses had accepted the idea of a general strike to destroy capitalist society). The *bourse du travail* movement petered out after 1900 and soon merged with the C.G.T., which had begun in 1895. But the C.G.T., though organized mainly on the basis of national industrial unions, had itself been captured by syndicalism. The statutes of the C.G.T. in 1903 included an effective if somewhat muted declaration of syndicalism: "[The C.G.T.] assembles, outside of any political tendency, all workers who are conscious of the struggle necessary for the disappearance of wage work and the employer class."

By 1900, syndicalism made sense to many French workers, and for a variety of reasons. This study, in showing that most French workers were neither revolutionary nor antipolitical, must contend that the importance of the causes of syndicalism have been exaggerated; but there were reasons to be revolutionary and antipolitical, and some workers were both.

Reasons for its Appeal

The most distinctive reason for a syndicalist stance lay clearly in the activities of the French government and the absence of a fully acceptable political alternative to it. The suppression of the Commune embittered many workers and proved that the republican government was nonetheless bourgeois and repressive. Long after the 1870s it was easy to see the government in this role. The French government, for all its commitment to political radicalism, was harsher or less sympathetic to workers than states such as Britain or Germany in one and perhaps two respects. Only Belgium, of the neighboring industrial countries, was more wedded to a repressive liberalism. The French government did not surround the industrial labor force with protective social insurance against illness, accidents, and old age, as most other states were doing in the latter nineteenth century. How much did this matter to the workers? Did they expect such protection and were they actively disgruntled by its absence? To some extent, perhaps; though it is worth noting that the first strike for social insurance occurred only in 1912. Doubtless French workers, like their counterparts in Germany, would have welcomed insurance plans and defended them once they were established; we cannot know how vigorously they resented the lack of systems which they had no experience of. And France's lag in social legislation should not be exaggerated. If there were no compulsory insurance schemes there were voluntary plans, run by the state, with several million participants.[2] Furthermore France led many industrial countries, including Belgium and Germany, in regulatory legislation over such matters as the hours of women in factories or of workers in the mines. Still, it can be argued that lack of state attention to some of labor's pressing needs helps explain the importance of syndicalism as a protest against the government.

It is possible also that French workers were subjected to the repressive force of the state more fully than were their counterparts elsewhere. In Paris, certainly, police supervision of union meetings, which included the introduction of spies into secret sessions and frequent arrests of union leaders, exceeded anything on record for any extended period of time, even in Germany. It is also true that France was the only industrial country which regularly sent military troops into mining and dock strikes; and this practice obviously contributed to syndicalism's resentment of the army. German and Belgian police were often much more brutal, with their cavalry charges against strike meetings and their bloody use of sabers on the unprotected heads of strikers; there is nothing in France to compare with the repression of the 1912 mining strike in the Ruhr, with its bloodshed and numerous arrests. On the other hand, there is nothing in France to compare with the German government's restraint in the 1905 Ruhr strike, in which no troops and only a few hundred extra police were sent in.

Two laws brought the French government directly into almost every strike. An 1848 ordinance allowed it to ban any meetings or demonstrations—yet without meetings few strikes could be called or maintained. The law was usually applied with tolerance, but meetings were often forbidden and some were vigorously attacked by the police.[3] More important still, the 1884 law that legalized strikes also barred violence or threats to induce workers to join strikes or to infringe upon the liberty of industry and work. During the railroad strike of 1910, strikers were even arrested for pointing at colleagues who were going to work.[4] Large numbers of strikers were jailed under these provisions as well as more general laws protecting property. The entire initial strike committee of the 1910 railroad strike was arrested for hindering the operation of trains. And arrests sometimes extended to the rank and file. During the railroad strike, 394 workers were arrested mainly for "intimidation" of nonstrikers; during a Paris bakers' strike 263 of at most 2,000 strikers were arrested, and there were many similar cases.[5]

It is difficult, of course, to compare police procedures. All industrial countries had laws similar to the French to circumscribe strikes; German legislation and, during the Taff Vale period, effective British legislation were tougher in some ways. Still in terms of enforcement, it is probable that the French police and military were more ubiquitous. Even aside from the big mining and dock strikes, which drew one soldier for every two or three strikers, smaller lockouts sometimes received an attention that has no parallel in other countries; fifty-five policemen were called in, for example, to patrol a strike by 150 weavers in one company in the Nord in 1903.[6] This sort of policy meant that every work site had a policeman present, that strike meetings were often ringed by police. If many strikers were intimidated as a result, many were deeply angered. The anger was probably all the greater in that the repression came from a government that French workers had once thought would be their own, for many of them or their fathers had been active republicans only a few decades before. They could not, like a German or Belgian militant, simply dismiss the government as a capitalist tool; it was this, but it had also betrayed their trust.[7]

Partly because of this sense that politics had deceived them, French workers might be suspicious of other political remedies. The nature of French socialism disillusioned some of them still further. In the first place, its more revolutionary strand, the Marxist group led by Jules Guesde, was authoritarian and inflexible. Its Marxist doctrine was imported anyway, and its stress on disciplined organization and political methods (Guesde had a distrust of unions and of strikes that was excessive even for Marxists) offended French labor traditions. It was in rebellion against Guesdist control of labor congresses and increasing efforts to take over the union movement that resolutions for a general strike began to be introduced in the 1880s; the C.G.T. was formed when a general strike resolution in 1894 led to the collapse of the Guesdist Federation of Syndicats. All of this simply widened the breach with socialism, for the Guesdists did not believe that strikes, whether general or partial, could have any significant success.

There were, of course, other types of socialism; indeed the very proliferation of groups and parties, with their conflicting claims and doctrines, may have alienated some workers from the political process. Most other socialist groups were reformists, who believed in evolution rather than revolution and who worked vigorously for limited but immediate social reforms. This approach naturally offered no satisfaction to workers who wanted to be revolutionary but could not accept Guesdist Marxism.

The entrance of a reformist socialist, Alexandre Millerand, into the "bourgeois" cabinet of 1899 shocked many workers who were not active revolutionaries. True, there was much initial enthusiasm for Millerand; few workers were so dogmatic as to reject co-operation with bourgeois politicians in principle. The electoral fortunes of the revolutionary Guesdist wing declined; thousands of strikers even in remote parts of the country appealed to Millerand for help, confident that, with him in the government, the state would be on their side. Much of this confidence was dispelled within a few years. The government did little more for workers than its predecessors had done; soldiers and police were still sent in to repress serious strikes. Many workers were clearly soured on politics, and the next years, from 1902 until 1907, saw the peak of syndicalist power in France.[8]

The political causes of syndicalism are reasonably clear. They do not tell us how many workers accepted the syndicalist approach but they do explain why many might have done so. But there is an economic explanation for syndicalism also, one which posits that the French labor force has enduring and distinctive characteristics. The argument might have two major stages: first, that unusual radicalism (if such indeed there was) was induced by unusual economic hardship in this period; second, that radicalism took a syndicalist form because of the peculiar, artisanal structure of French manufacturing.

There were certainly many reasons for French workers to complain about the state of the economy from the 1890s onward, and some of these reasons were new. The unemployment rate was surprisingly high, though this has escaped the notice of most historians of the period. It was a bit lower than in Britain but significantly above German and Belgian levels. According to union figures, average annual unemployment never fell below 7% between 1901 and 1909. There was a distinct drop thereafter (to 4.2% in 1911), which helps explain the decline in syndicalist enthusiasm in those years. Certainly the previous high levels helped motivate protest.[9] In industries such as the building trades, where syndicalism was particularly strong, the relation between unemployment and radical protest is clear. A slump in employment from 1901 to 1905 was followed by sufficient improvement to allow a massive wave of strikes, notably the C.G.T.-led outburst in 1906. The goals of these and other strikes, particularly in metalwork and the crafts, were shaped in part by the pressure that periodic unemployment put upon working conditions. The number of workers was increasing in France at a time when technical improvements in many industries curtailed the demand for labor. Complaints about female workers and misuse of apprentices directly reflected the insecurity and discontent of workers as diverse as bakers and riveters. Also, skilled workers who were driven to seek occasional employment as stevedores or ditchdiggers sometimes imposed their radicalism on unskilled workers, who had traditionally been more apathetic. There was a great opportunity for syndicalism here.[10]

Trends of wages and prices most directly spurred working-class grievance during the prewar period. They contradicted workers' hopes and expectations and may have led to an absolute deterioration in conditions for important groups in the labor force. There is a complication here. Historians and most contemporary observers (from outside the working class) have erred in describing the trend in real wages. Their error is important. It distorts the picture of workers' aspirations. But it can be used to explain the rise of syndicalism. I must describe different trends, which I think are still more compatible with the effervescence of protest. But I'll hedge my bets, since resolution of the issue is not indispensable for an understanding of syndicalism. I will describe the conventional view and its implications and then turn to the refutation and its implications. In this matter the reader can have the cake of custom and eat it too.[11]

The conventional picture shows money wages rising steadily, by 10% between 1900 and 1910. Expenses increased also, particularly after 1905; by 1910 they were 4% above the 1900 level. The obvious result was a comfortable increase in real wages, of 4.5% by 1905, 6% by 1910.[12] Jürgen Kuczynski, the German Marxist historian, who cannot be accused of willingly exaggerating working-class gains, has on the whole accepted this pattern. He admits an 8% improvement in real wages by 1910, followed by a definite decline hereafter; real wages dropped below 1900 levels in 1912 and stood only 5% above them in 1914.[13]

This is compatible with an understanding of the outburst of worker protest and of syndicalism after 1900. The improvements in real wages were not as rapid as in previous decades, while expectation had perhaps increased. The rise in prices may have created a sense of deterioration even where none existed. Furthermore, any modest gains that workers had made by 1910 were eclipsed by the huge increase in industrial profits. Total corporate revenue rose rapidly; even in 1909, a recession year, it stood 24% above 1901 levels. In mining, where productivity per worker declined slightly, wage costs fell in relation to prices (which were rising) from 49.6% in 1901 to 48.1% in 1910; here was greater margin for the capitalists. In industries such as metallurgy, benefits from improved productivity went almost exclusively to the entrepreneurs. Labor's share in total industrial income was declining rapidly.[14] Hence syndicalists and other radicals, who urged the necessity of rapidly rising standards of living and railed against unfair profits, had ample potential appeal.

In actuality, however, the evolution of real wages in the period was more directly menacing to many workers than the conventional picture implies. Money wages rose, but prices rose much faster. Patterns varied from industry to industry, and the important category of textile workers suffered stagnation even in wages; but overall, workers' monetary pay probably rose 12% from 1900 to 1910.[15] Prices, however, when adjusted for the actual importance of each item in working-class budgets, increased 13% to 14%; the rise in food prices alone added 12.5% to the total cost of living by 1910. As a result, workers were forced to curtail their standards of living. By 1911, they were spending 22% of their budget on meats, on the average, instead of 26% as in 1907, despite the increase in meat prices. Instead, they bought more bread. In another important adjustment, working-class families became more dependent on the earnings of their children, for one survey revealed that children's contributions to total family income nearly doubled as a percentage of total income between 1907 and 1914.[16]

Workers, then, were becoming poorer, at least until 1910; only in the four years before World War I did real incomes rise once more. This certainly helps to explain the appeal of syndicalism. Workers were radicalized by deteriorating conditions; when the deterioration stopped after 1910 the appeal of syndicalism waned. It is worth noting also that conditions in Germany and perhaps in Belgium, though considerably worse than in France, probably improved in this period; this helps explain why nothing so radical as syndicalism developed in these countries.[17] On the other hand, standards of living fell even more rapidly in Britain, particularly after 1910, without bringing on any massive syndicalist movement; this suggests some comparative problems to which we shall return. Finally, though slightly increasing hardship may explain the rise of syndicalism, it also raises a major problem of interpretation. Syndicalists urged workers to battle for positive improvements in their conditions, while workers faced a struggle simply to keep what they already had. Here was a potentially important gap between what leaders meant by the syndicalist movement and what ordinary workers had in mind.

Unemployment and at best stagnating real wages caused a mounting wave of protest after 1900; about this there can be little disagreement. The more complex question is whether the structure of the French economy channeled the protest in a distinctive, syndicalist direction. The familiar point is that France was less completely industrialized than Germany or Britain, and her firms were smaller. This structure in turn encouraged a labor movement whose organization and goals were both decentralized. Workers could not easily establish a tightly organized union movement because factories were small and dispersed, and tight organization was unnecessary because their employers, too, were individualistic and weakly organized. Finally, large numbers of workers were artisans and sought a movement that would express their hopes for a local, producer-controlled economy.

French artisans faced something of a crisis at the end of the nineteenth century, aside from specific developments in wages or levels of employment. Mechanization spread to almost all trades, often for the first time. In the manufacture of shoes and hats, big, mechanized plants came to dominate production after 1900, displacing many artisans and forcing others, such as cutters and mounters in the shoe factories, to use new methods. Mechanical kneading machines were introduced in baking; construction firms used mechanical cranes for lifting, and mechanical saws. At the same time, the size of companies in the traditional trades increased. In all branches of the construction industry, units with less than twenty workers declined in absolute numbers, while all categories of larger firms expanded. Between 1896 and 1906, the number of small masonry contractors in Paris declined by 160, while the number of employers with over one hundred workers more than doubled. Similar trends were at work in baking, metalwork, and many other craft industries.[18]

So the familiar argument about the French economy can be made more subtle for this period. Syndicalism may have reflected not only the enduring character of much French manufacturing, but also a rather new challenge to this character. Artisanal forms were remembered, the average firm was still small enough to permit a loosely organized protest movement, but conditions were changing. Syndicalism would not have been the first movement by small shopworkers to protest industrialization in the name of tradition, but in most industrial countries the time for this sort of protest had long since passed.

Were the conditions of French artisans distinctive enough to support syndicalism? Outside the traditional crafts, in industries such as textiles or metallurgy, firms were larger and mechanization long established. To be sure, the average company was smaller than firms in similar industries in Germany or Britain, and perhaps workers even in these industries remained attracted to goals of localism and small shop organization, which syndicalism could have expressed. But workers in these industries were hardly artisans, and textile workers, whose firms were the smallest and most dispersed and who were unusually numerous in the French labor force, were among the groups most immune to syndicalism. So for the French labor force as a whole, claims of general characteristics derived from small units of organization need some qualification at least.

There may have been, however, general characteristics of the labor policies of French employers which explain the applicability of syndicalism to groups of workers who were in no sense artisans. From a comparative standpoint, despite many individual and industrial variations, French employers stand out in the years around 1900 as being at once unusually harsh and unusually ineffective in their relations with workers. They were much less conciliatory and less open to collective bargaining than most British industrialists; they were reluctant to treat workers on any basis of equality. In this they resembled the bigger German manufacturers; but unlike the Germans they did not organize effectively to quash labor protest.

When French employers dealt with strikers, personal animosity often came to the surface. In a strike by fishermen in Sète, the wife of one employer threw slops on a worker demonstration, while another made vulgar gestures. A mine director in Hénin-Liétard (Nord) shouted to strikers: "If I had twenty policemen, how I would attack you bastards." [19] More general policies against labor agitation reflected similar sentiments. Angry employers fired all or some of their strikers, sometimes recruiting strike-breaking toughs from the several organizations that supplied such people.[20] The increasing duration of the average strike during the 1890s revealed how bitterly many employers held out against concessions. More indicative still was the common resistance to formal negotiation, especially when unions were involved. French manufacturers were extremely jealous of their power and often feared bargaining as an "abdication of all authority . . . of all responsibility." [21] Even when they did negotiate they often refused to sign any agreement. They exceeded even their German counterparts in their reluctance to admit workers to any share in policy. Insofar as syndicalism was an unusually radical and direct protest against employer authority, the policies of French manufacturers help explain it.

Syndicalism was also possible in France because of the weakness of French employers; even loosely organized unions had a good chance against them. Only in a few industries, notably glass manufacture and metallurgy, were manufacturers strong enough to silence protest regularly. French industry as a whole showed few of the signs of effective toughness visible in Germany in the period. Rates of success in strikes were quite high in France until 1906. Average strikes were much shorter in France than in Germany, which reflected the French employers' inability to hold out. Lockouts were far less common in France than in Belgium or Germany, where they averaged about 10% of the strike rate. Employer associations arose only slowly in France. To be sure, their membership increased from 151,624 in 1899 to 421,566 in 1913; but even in 1913 most employers were unorganized and most organizations were quite loose.[22] This was what made syndicalist methods realistic in part, until after 1906 at least. A broader question remains: were not these methods, abstracted from syndicalist doctrine, used by workers everywhere in the early stages of the labor movement and adopted in France after 1900, not because of unusual traditions or radicalism, but simply because employers had yet to challenge them effectively?

Taken in combination, the various explanations of syndicalism, both political and economic, are more than plausible. They have been used by serious students of French labor and will doubtless continue to be used. And they may account for many leading features of the French labor movement.

Chief Manifestations

The most obvious manifestation of syndicalism in practice continued well after 1900 to be the resolutions of the C.G.T. and many member unions. In the 1906 C.G.T. Congress, in Amiens, efforts by the socialist leader of the textile federation to combine political with economic action and to push for legislated social reforms were defeated. The Congress resolved overwhelmingly that a new society was possible only "through the struggles of workers in the economic sphere." [23] Other speakers condemned nationalism and the army, urging increasingly bold "antimilitarist and antipatriotic propaganda." The 1908 Congress discussed a general strike and insurrection in case of war. The 1910 Congress repeated the antimilitarist declaration, while the 1912 Congress reaffirmed faith in syndicalist methods alone, noting again that socialists were not revolutionaries. Pursuant to resolutions of this sort, the C.G.T. set up, in 1900, a general strike committee and thereafter disseminated a variety of pamphlets on the general strike and on sabotage and other direct-action methods.

Among leaders of the C.G.T. and of major union federations such as
metal and construction and among many local organizers as well,
syndicalism flourished until 1914 and beyond. To be sure, the Congress
votes were misleading in many ways. Each individual union federation
had the same vote, regardless of the size of membership. This meant that
the vote of the vigorously syndicalist barbers' union, with 2,300 members
in 1910, was equal to the vote of the giant, largely reformist, railroad
workers' federation, with 50,000 members. All efforts by reformists to
obtain a voting system that would reflect union size were defeated. Still,
the Congress votes for syndicalist resolutions were massive; in 1912, for
example, the antisocialist motion was carried by 1,057 to 35. This does
not, of course, automatically assure us that the rank and file shared the
same enthusiasm.

Membership figures may take us a step further. In 1902, 122,000 workers of all sorts belonged to the C.G.T. This rose to 300,000 in 1906 and
to 600,000 in 1912. Such a large increase can be misleading. The final
figure, at least, was in some senses inflated, for only 450,000 of the members regularly paid dues; there is no doubt that the C.G.T.'s growth rate
slowed considerably after 1906. Furthermore, the C.G.T.'s share of all
unionized French workers did not rise as rapidly as its overall membership. The jump from 20% in 1902 to 37% in 1906 was significant but is no
decisive proof of syndicalism's attractiveness. (In 1912, over 55% of all
unionized workers were in the C.G.T., if the figure of 600,000 members
is accepted.) And membership figures do not reveal reasons for joining.
Unions were growing all over industrial Europe. Was the C.G.T.'s growth
due simply to its existence as an organization, or did its syndicalist pronouncements play a great role? Accounts of the French labor movement
typically assume that syndicalism repelled enough workers to slow trade-
union growth in France, in comparison with its growth in Britain or
Germany, but that C.G.T. members must have been positively attracted:
hence the significance of the rapid increase in membership. But the
assumption of correspondence between members and leaders is just that—
without further positive symptoms of syndicalist influence.

Many features of French union organization were consistent with the
syndicalist approach. This resulted, in part at least, from the promptings
of the leaders; but many scholars have argued that it reflected workers'
desires as well and that union structure proved that syndicalism sprang
from the character of the French labor force. The history of union
financing is most commonly cited. Compared to British or German
unions, French unions were poor. They were slow to develop benefit

funds for illness or old age; they did not produce the massive publications and investigations of labor conditions that their counterparts elsewhere did. Many local unions, like the Seine locksmiths during the 1890s, had no significant benefit program at all: they only made occasional grants to widows of members, and these in no predetermined amount. Syndicalists distrusted wealthy unions, for their wealth might induce attachment to the existing order and a conservative approach generally (groups like the printers' federation that were well-financed were indeed unusually cautious). They wanted a sleek combat unit. And many French workers responded to this approach. They, too, saw the union as a fighting organization. Individualistic to the core, they resisted any organization that tried to bind them too closely or to charge high dues; ironically, many of them resisted even the syndicalist leaders when they began gradually to raise the dues. Here, so the common argument runs, is proof that true syndicalism, before it bogged down in bureaucracy, and the French worker reinforced each other, that they saw the conditions for effective action in the same way. Other factors can be added. The small size of the average union, with only 170 members in 1905, reflected France's decentralized industry but also perhaps the persistent localism of French workers. Frequent challenges to union leaders, which in some syndicalist unions produced a stipulation that no leader could serve more than a single term, reveal the deep-seated desire for labor democracy.

These symptoms of syndicalism cannot be lightly dismissed, but they raise a host of questions. There is no doubt that the syndicalist leaders' concepts of the purposes of a union differed from prevailing ideas in Britain and Germany; though it must be noted that German unions had vigorous quarrels about whether benefit funds would weaken the fighting spirit of unions and that the French themselves steadily elaborated benefit programs (and correspondingly increased union dues, which tripled between 1900 and 1914). But did the French workers' attitudes toward unions really dispose them, distinctively, to a syndicalist approach? Workers everywhere in this period sought to defend or increase union democracy and to preserve the power of small, local unions. Battles for such causes loom large in British and German union history in the period, and syndicalism had little to do with them. Correspondingly, it is doubtful that unions in France had a greater turnover in leadership, at least at the top, than elsewhere; though it is certainly true that they had smaller central bureaucracies.

The question of union financing and dues involves comparable problems. German workers (who in terms of national character are supposed to be disciplined and well-organized) were not syndicalist; but they were, like most French workers (and unlike the British), rather new to the union movement. German union dues were, per capita, not much higher than French in the late 1890s. They then rose much more rapidly, largely because union leaders, not being syndicalists and faced with far more strenuous employer opposition, pushed the matter harder. Ordinary German workers resisted vigorously, simply because they were poor and unaccustomed to such obligations. Only gradually did they accept high dues, in part because the benefit programs their leaders established and widely publicized showed their utility. During most of the prewar years, German individualism in union matters was in many ways greater than French. Most notably, German unions annually faced a membership turnover of 100% or more; that is, typically, as many members left the union as had been in it when the year began, though some members joined and quit the union in the same year and an important nucleus of more durable members remained. Though precise figures are lacking, it is doubtful that French unions encountered individual fickleness in so extreme a form. In one specific case, that of the French metalworkers' union between 1909 and 1911, turnover occurred at only two-thirds the rate of the German metalworkers' federation. In resisting higher dues and, sometimes, in quitting their union, French workers were not behaving in a necessarily distinctive fashion, particularly since their leaders were often slow to urge otherwise.[24]

It can be suggested, then, that some of the features of French unions generally cited as indicative or supportive of syndicalism were not as unusual as is generally claimed by historians of France alone and that they did not derive from any special characteristics of French labor. The theory is not, however, destroyed. Among other things, sufficient experience with syndicalist unions may have made many French workers angry, antiorganization men. Lack of adequate strike funds due to union poverty embittered workers in strike after strike; some turned against the unions as a result, while others blamed the capitalist order and some became increasingly violent. At the least, French workers in many unions had no substantial benefit programs to act as a taming influence. Even in this regard, the importance of those unions that were not of the syndicalist type must be stressed. The printers' federation and the provincial construction unions established high dues and benefit programs comparable to those elsewhere well before 1900.

Role in Strikes

The advocate of the importance of syndicalism can complete his argument by noting at least some of the characteristics of the French strike movement in the syndicalist period, from the mid-nineties to World War I. (Few students of syndicalism have, however, developed this argument, beyond references to a few individual strikes, because of their preoccupation with formal union organization and resolutions.) The balance of this study will attempt to show that strike patterns prove that French workers were not effectively syndicalist; but there is some serious evidence to the contrary.

Within France, the tactics of syndicalist unions differed greatly, at least on paper, from those of reformist unions. Statutes of the moderate railroad federation and the northern miners' federation, for example, insisted that workers try conciliation procedures before any strike and undertake no effort without approval of at least two-thirds of the membership. They worked for realistic demands that could be won without total conflict with management. The northern miners rejected a syndicalist appeal to campaign for eight hours and eight francs a day in favor of lower wage demands that would not compromise the claim for reduced hours. The printers' federation similarly sought nine instead of eight hours in 1906. Always the emphasis was on bargaining and ironclad contracts that could be observed by both sides. The printers, for example, strove for rates of maximum hours and minimum pay, but they promised their employers a minimum production in return.[25] It was Auguste Keufer, the head of the printers' federation, who summed up the reformist spirit most clearly: "We seriously want what we demand, we must act with a great prudence combined with a vigorous will; we are the instrument of action that it took 25 years of effort to create; we must use it with foresight without risking its destruction."[26] In sum, reformist unions in France intended to act as the major union movements of other industrial countries intended.

At its most extreme, the syndicalist impulse was to substitute vigor for organization in strike activity, and it looked to the individual strike as a forerunner of, a kind of primary-school training for, the general strike.[27] The syndicalist approach colored the rhetoric of a strike and sometimes affected conduct. Some leaders advocated violence, not only against disloyal workers but also against the police and employers. After the police killed a striker in Villeneuve-Saint Georges in 1908, the C.G.T.

organized a demonstration in Paris and at least indirectly incited the 6,000 demonstrators to attack the omnipresent police and army.[28] A syndicalist in a dockers' strike in La Palliers urged the workers to "break the faces" of strikebreakers and to throw acid at the troops, for "gentlemen and horses will dance at this." [29] The most consistent advocacy of direct violence occurred during the strikes by food workers, whose leaders were fervently syndicalist and whose strike efforts were usually weak. The head of the waiters' union recommended putting drugs in food "in such a way as to give more or less violent colic to all the bourgeois eating in the restaurant."[30] Such promptings often bore fruit. A leader of the leather-workers in Lyons shouted, "All will go well when two or three employers have been hanged," [31] and some factories were stoned after this meeting. Several strike meetings in Paris led directly to attacks on the police, particularly before 1909; so did the syndicalist-led ditchdiggers' strike in Aix-en-Provence as late as 1913.[32]

Syndicalist leaders were sometimes tempted to prolong strikes. A representative of the metallurgical federation, one Gautier, urged Hennebont strikers to persevere: "We don't want to return like this; our dignity orders us to carry on lest we insult the whole proletariat." [33] Syndicalists were often loath to bargain. The barbers' federation long resisted collective contracts lest they limit workers' freedom to protest when they wished.[34] Raymond Péricat, of the building trades' federation, expressed a general sentiment: "A contract is signed only between people who want to make peace. There is no peace to be made between exploiter and exploited." [35]

Above all, syndicalist leaders sought to use strikes to promote the later general rising. Pamphlets were distributed; 50,000 copies of Aristide Briand's book on the general strike were passed out in the Montceau miners' strike of 1901.[36] Strike meetings were used to educate the workers. A leader of Toulon arsenal workers shouted in 1909: "The social edifice will be demolished only by our arms and our tools." [37] A delegate from the building trades' federation told striking painters, in Montpellier: "Present society is a wall of granite which the exploited should overturn; its pillars are parliamentarism, the army, the courts, and capital." [38] A man named Sorrel, head of the Grenoble cabinetmakers' union, told his charges during a strike: "If they oppose us with bullets, we'll answer with bullets; if they strike us, we'll hit back, for we'll be defending ourselves legitimately and we'll take by force the factories which belong to us, for we built them." [39] Two days later, 5,000 workers gathered before the plant of a particularly recalcitrant manufacturer and stoned it and the troops around it; briefly, the following day, barricades were set up.

A syndicalist-led strike could, then, be quite different from a reformist effort. The biggest difference lay in what was said during the strike; even recommendations of violence were often a bit abstract, pointed more toward a general strike than toward any present agitation. Because of their attachment to economic weapons and their fundamental radicalism, syndicalists could play on the excitement of a strike situation more fully than socialists, who tended to attack the existing order in more elaborate and erudite terms. Did this lead to distinctive action? Did it induce a longer-term commitment to syndicalism? What actual features of French strikes in general show any relationship to a distinctively syndicalist approach?

First of all, there is the coincidence between the rapidly rising strike rate and the advance of syndicalism. The relationship between syndicalism and the huge increase in strikes between 1902 and 1907 may be quite specific. It was in 1902 that syndicalist leaders began to pay explicit attention to fomenting strikes directly, and during the five or six years thereafter the revolutionary ardor of syndicalist leadership was at a peak. Obviously this, along with other factors, bears some relationship to the increasing strike rate; the question is, how much, particularly given the small number of syndicalist leaders and the fact that most strikes began without formal direction at all. We are back again to the question of the extent to which syndicalist ideology or impulse had spread among French workers. And was the stabilization of the strike rate after 1910 due to the decline of revolutionary enthusiasm among the chiefs of the C.G.T.?

The years 1899–1914 constitute a peak in strike activity according to several criteria that might be relevant to syndicalism. The comparison applies not only to earlier labor protest but also to subsequent twentieth-century French experience. There were more strikes in an average year than ever before or than occurred afterward, until 1945, except in an individual year or two of crisis, like 1919 and 1920. Between 1921 and 1929 the average number of strikes declined notably, to 825 a year. There were more strikers on the average, but this simply means that the prewar years constituted the heyday of small, loosely organized but frequent strikes. And despite the increased number of strikers, the average number of working days lost each year in strikes dropped significantly, from 4,107,000 to 3,922,600. Strikes became better organized and thus larger on the average; but the intensity of grievance either diminished or was

better controlled by labor organizations, so strikes became less frequent
and lasted a shorter time.[40] In other words, strike patterns before World
War I may have been formed by syndicalist tactics and union organization or by spontaneous outbursts by radical workers in sympathy with
syndicalism, or both.

The actual origins of most strikes confirm this estimate in part, though
they complicate claims of direct syndicalist inspiration. Spontaneity played
an important role even in large strikes, such as the railroad strike of 1910.
As a tactic, spontaneity made sense to many workers because it caught
employers off guard and brought possible victory without elaborate
preparation or organization; this was clearly akin to the syndicalist
spirit. Workers often believed that surprise was their best weapon, that
any warning or prior effort to negotiate or organize simply gave the
employer a chance to fire them. In 1910 a textile union in La Gorgue-
Estaires (Nord) circulated a wage demand to various manufacturers; it
had no desire to strike. But the workers, fearing that the employers would
stall and finish the work in course and so be prepared to resist a strike,
grew excited and walked out on their own. But spontaneity resulted
from more than a sense of tactics. Many strikes occurred because workers felt so much frustration and hostility that these simply had to find an
outlet. Sometimes the subsequent strike demands inadequately conveyed
the emotion involved, which was too deep to formulate precisely. Indeed,
some spontaneous strikes began with no demands at all, partly because
workers feared to draw up a list lest they disclose their agitation prematurely and partly because their grievances were so sweeping that no
negotiable list could sum them up. Some spontaneous strikes, then,
resulted from a pent-up emotion that really amounted to a rebellion,
however local, against the existing system. Workers in such strikes may
well have been syndicalists or open to syndicalist appeal.[41]

Many strikes of newly unionized workers were essentially spontaneous
and revealed the indirect influence of syndicalist promptings. Union
leaders stirred up the expectations which led to a strike, but they neither
called nor initially led the walkout itself. The experience of the slateworkers' federation was typical. A major organizing effort followed the
establishment of the national union in 1904. Newly recruited local leaders
and many other members viewed the union as a weapon of war and
began raising exaggerated demands; interestingly, the demands were
largely personal, concerning dismissed workers, and the result was a
series of strikes no better organized than a nonunion effort. The slateworkers' federation was vigorously syndicalist; its propaganda may well

have prepared the workers for strikes that were essentially bursts of anger rather than realistic efforts to win precise gains. But this example reveals also the tenuousness of the link between syndicalism and the spontaneous strike movement; the slateworkers' strikes were resisted by the federation because they were doomed to failure and therefore threatened the organization. So the question is, did syndicalism really cause the spontaneous element so common in French strikes? Or was spontaneity natural to workers who were inexperienced in industrial conflict and impatient for results? An intermediate position is possible, too. Syndicalism may not have caused the spontaneous element but its doctrines, preached for example when new unions were formed, may have encouraged workers to believe that a sudden walkout was the best way to tackle an employer, while its decentralized union structure and radical leaders delayed any effective effort to control spontaneity.

Syndicalist unions definitely encouraged spontaneity in one respect, at least until 1910. They rarely insisted on a careful strike vote by relevant workers before a strike began. A few syndicalist unions had provisions for consultation before a strike, but there was none of the elaborate constitutional apparatus characteristic of British and German unions, or of the reformist unions in France, where not only strikes but even peaceful pay demands required advance authorization from the central federation. Where votes were taken, before or during a strike, they typically occurred during a meeting, which was more likely to be attended by the most radical workers than by the general mass; and the voting was by voice, which made it difficult for a moderate but timid soul to object to a strike.[42] British workers who visited France were deeply offended by this undemocratic and, in their eyes, tactically unwise procedure. But it corresponded to the syndicalist desire for loose organization in which, without denying democracy directly, the radical minority would win out. (A similar principle was, after all, involved in the method of voting in the C.G.T. congresses, which assured a radical majority of those present but one unrepresentative of the membership as a whole.) And this arrangement corresponded to what the more active French workers wanted, at least during the excitement of a strike.[43]

The spontaneity of many strikes and the absence of advance consultation, both encouraged by syndicalism to some extent at least, explain the small size as well as the frequency of French strikes in general. The issues involved were too immediate and narrow, the lack of preparation too obvious, to command widespread support. Among workers actually affected by the immediate grievance, participation was typically high, but it was difficult to spread the effort beyond them. Hence the average strike was small and affected few companies. Between 1899 and 1914, in fact, the average strike involved only 239 workers; and 74% of all strikes affected only one company. Workers thought and acted in terms of their own firm in their own locality and, often, among workers of their own skill or profession alone. Syndicalism, which preached working-class unity, did not create this framework; but the framework may show why French workers were drawn to a movement that was loosely and locally organized both at the time and in its future goals.

Significantly, strikes that went beyond the usual framework were more often city-wide, cutting across industrial lines, than industry-wide and national. Here the strong local bent of syndicalist leaders and of many workers is clearly revealed. General local strikes occurred in Dunkerque, Mazamet, Voiron, Le Havre, and twice in Marseilles; the 1906 strike for an eight-hour day, which the C.G.T. organized, had something of this same quality (particularly in Paris, where up to 100,000 workers struck), for agitation tended to follow local rather than industrial lines. These strikes were quite large during their brief peak; in August or September of 1900, 49,650 workers were out in Marseilles. And the percentage of participation was often high as well: almost all the 4,560 printing, textile, metallurgical and transport workers joined in the Mazamet strike of September 1910.[44] There were strikes of this kind in other countries, of course, particularly (as in France) in port cities, where a dockers' strike could affect workers of all sorts. The 1911 strike in Liverpool, for example, had much the same character as efforts in Marseilles or Le Havre. It is not even possible to argue that there were more local general strikes in France than in Britain. But what is clear is that French workers, though ready for an intensive local effort on occasions, resisted industry-wide strikes of the sort that became common in Britain. Only miners, merchant seamen, and, to a more limited extent, dock workers could spread their agitation. The 1910 railroad strike, though it affected several areas, confirmed the difficulty of this sort of effort. Syndicalist union organization was too weak for a national strike (most of the national movements were directed by at least partially nonsyndicalist leadership); they could not, like the British in 1911 and 1912, extend local strikes into national ones. And perhaps something in the character of the French labor force, to which syndicalism appealed, inhibited the carefully coordinated national strike as well.[45]

Spontaneity and the pervasive localism were the most important similarities between syndicalism and overall strike tactics in France. There were several other distinctive syndicalist strike tactics that deserve mention; they were less widely accepted by French workers and even where accepted were often resented. For some groups, however, they may indicate a correspondence between special interests of French workers and syndicalism.

The strikes conducted by most French unions, whether syndicalist or not, were unusually badly financed. This followed, of course, from the poverty of the unions as a whole. Strike payments in France were lower than in Britain or Germany; only the printers, who paid three and a half to four francs a day to members (over half of normal salary) approached levels common in other countries among skilled workers. Several metalworkers' groups promised two francs a day to all striking members, but they rarely provided it. The metalworkers' federation gave an average of half a franc a day to strikers it aided in 1909. The building trades' federation did not even set up a strike fund until 1908, though some local unions in the federation had one earlier; most striking Parisian construction workers received no formal aid at all.[46] Furthermore some unions, particularly in the building trades, did not encourage their members to seek work elsewhere, unlike German unions which required single workers to leave town in a long strike. Syndicalist leaders differed on this matter, but many urged that all workers should remain on hand to demonstrate and to show the power and radicalism of labor. Workers often disobeyed and left anyway, but when they did not they put a further burden on inadequate strike funds.

Inadequate strike funds often caused great resentment among French workers. The inadequacy helps explain why many French strikes were small (in comparison to those in Britain, for example) and short (in comparison to those in Germany). The real misery workers suffered during long strikes sometimes led them to violence. In other words some features of the French strike movement that seem to be syndicalist may owe more to syndicalist financial policies than to any special characteristics of French labor. But these policies may also have induced a more far-reaching interaction between French workers and syndicalism.

In contrast to British and especially German workers, the French worker on strike depended on active local solidarity more than on any other source. Strikers had to solicit support from their fellows in bars, on the streets, and in factories. Armentières workers, contributing on a factory by factory basis, gave 14,204 francs to Lille textile strikers in 1904. In the 1912 Paris taxi strike, drivers who worked were assessed five francs a day, which yielded at least 12,000 francs daily. Similar efforts occurred in other countries, of course, but less frequently. The local collections in France (unlike the national collections for a few prominent strikes, which took place no oftener in France than elsewhere) may have reflected and encouraged a sense of solidarity in combat that was related to syndicalism.

By 1906 the favorite syndicalist tactic in a long strike, rare in other industrial countries, was the "communist soup." Using gifts of food, often city facilities, and outright cash, strikers could be provided two meals for .30–.45 francs a day if fed by collective kitchens. By this means workers and especially their wives learned the virtues of collective effort; "communist soups" were excellent devices to keep spirits up and spread syndicalist propaganda. They were widely used in factory towns. But there were drawbacks. Many housewives, the eternal enemy of strikes and syndicalism, resented the infringements on privacy. Mismanagement of the soups was often charged; the Graulhet leatherworkers' union had to parade some cattle in the streets in 1909 to refute accusations that the soup was getting thinner. The system almost never worked in Paris or in other big cities, even where many workers were syndicalists.[47]

One other tactic was dictated both by syndicalist strategy and by the necessities of strikes in France. To spread and to maintain a strike, urban strikers often organized a "fox hunt" (*chasse aux renards*), sending groups of about fifteen workers from shop to shop to announce a strike and also to break tools and even heads if necessary. Syndicalist leaders, particularly in the building trades, urged such tactics vigorously, for solidarity had to be enforced. Some of them undoubtedly urged attacks on nonstrikers more frequently and more violently than their counterparts in Britain and certainly in Germany. Because strikes in France were so often spontaneous and badly organized, involving a radical minority trying to compel a reluctant majority, violent tactics of this sort were in some ways especially necessary. Here is another possible similarity between syndicalism and the real radicalism of a segment of French labor; the only trouble is that it is not clear that, despite the incitement, attacks on nonstrikers were any more frequent or violent in France than elsewhere.[48]

By 1900 almost every segment of the French labor force was in a mood to protest at least occasionally. Textile workers struck repeatedly against stagnating wages; coal miners rebelled more often than any other group. Skilled artisans, long a bulwark of protest movements, had new grievances in the changing economy; and the unskilled workers, particularly on the docks, were awakening for the first time.

Syndicalist leaders and organizations were in the thick of the fight. Three major unions were thoroughly syndicalist throughout the period: the construction workers, metalworkers, and the national miners' federation (the separate miners' union in the biggest French basin, in the Nord and Pas-de-Calais, was reformist). In moments of particular stress, especially around Paris, important segments of unions like the printers' federation and the railroad workers' federation developed syndicalist leadership. Small unions in less well-organized trades, like the bakers' and barbers' federations, were vigorously syndicalist. And syndicalist leaders played a big role in strikes by other groups, even in remote areas, such as the 1905 metallurgical workers' strike in Lorraine and strikes by silk workers in the south.

Syndicalists had good reason to hope for broad support. Artisans, particularly in Paris, shared many of the traditions from which syndicalism sprang. They provided the most vigorous support for the C.G.T. and must not be overlooked in a general assessment of syndicalism's influence on workers. But many other types of workers were susceptible to the vigor and immediacy of syndicalism. Workers stirring in factory cities under the heavy hand of an authoritarian employer and unskilled laborers faced with enormous barriers against protests were among the hundreds of thousands who welcomed syndicalist assistance.

The symptoms of syndicalism in union structure and strike activity were significant. A good half of France's union leaders, local as well as national, were led by their fervent syndicalist beliefs not to undertake or to undertake only reluctantly organizational measures that were common elsewhere. We must constantly try to isolate this negative influence of syndicalism, its failure to restrain workers' normal impulses, from its positive role in setting goals and tactics. But many elements of the political and economic structure encouraged a positive role as well. It is time for a more thorough test of syndicalism's influence.

2 The Moderation of French Workers

No historian can claim certain knowledge of what French workers wanted in the years before World War I. It would be convenient if they wanted what their leaders said they should want, but this is precisely what needs investigating. Happily an assessment of the methods the workers used in protest largely confirms my contention that they really wanted what they themselves said they wanted.

Strikes, of course, measure what workers judge tactically feasible, not what they might ultimately hope for. To be sure, many strikes in France began in a spontaneous burst of anger, and it is interesting that, as we shall see, the angriest strikes produced quite limited demands. Still, strikes were, for all their excitement, difficult and risky ventures, and few workers plunged into them without some sense of what was realistically possible. In suggesting that the desires of workers differed from those of syndicalist leaders we are saying, in part, that their sense of the possible differed. Furthermore, strikes, as a form of protest, tend to fall to the lowest common denominator in demands. That is, strikes depend on widespread support in the relevant work group, and both leaders and ordinary strikers realize this. An ardent minority, then, often moderates its goals or is forced to do so in the interests of spreading and winning a strike. This often happened in France. One of the reasons for the high incidence of wage demands was that these appealed to almost all workers, whether mildly aggrieved or bitterly angry, whether really concerned about their pay or primarily worried about the introduction of new machines (for which a raise might, however inadequately, have compensated). The usual goals of strikes concealed minority-majority divisions, just as they glossed over crucial regional and industrial variations. Many of the atypical workers may have been convinced syndicalists; some undoubtedly were. But at the very least, an examination of strike goals reveals that syndicalists were a minority of the minority of those workers who protested at all. Because of this they could not dominate strikes and syndicalist leaders could not let them try.

Most strikes were not formally led by syndicalists. They either had no union guidance at all or occurred in industries in which the unions were not syndicalist. The textile industry, in which syndicalist influence was limited, produced the largest number of strikes; coal mining, particularly in the reformist north, produced the largest number of strikers. This helps explain the lack of correspondence between syndicalist goals and strike demands. But even in the syndicalist unions, actual strike demands differed little from national patterns. Strikes in industries where syndicalist unions were strong, such as metals, were frequently spontaneous and produced their own demands before the unions took over tactical control. Even syndicalist campaigns were sometimes turned to other purposes by the strikers; this repeatedly occurred during agitation for reduction of hours of work in the construction industry, that bulwark of syndicalist unionism. French workers either did not have revolutionary hopes, at least outside the political arena, or they were overawed by the practical barriers. Indeed, the class as a whole was reluctant to press even for immediate major reforms.

This reluctance stands out in the period. A comparative framework suggests that it was not the tactical barriers that deterred more far-reaching protest, but the lack of far-reaching goals. Though French workers did not strike for political purposes, workers from Spain to Russia were doing so regularly, sometimes under syndicalist guidance and in a far more repressive environment. Political strikes or riots occurred in Belgium and Germany, more comparable industrial countries; in Germany they were even partially spontaneous. But in France, with a syndicalist movement primed to lead political strikes (for strikes against the state required a political consciousness), almost nothing happened. The main reason was that French workers did not suffer the political disabilities that Italian and German workers did; they had no need for massive suffrage strikes like those in Belgium. But the absence of political protests, in an age of political unrest elsewhere, also indicates that the mass of French workers, including the especially aggrieved, paid little heed to the long-range goals of syndicalism. Again, we cannot prove that they did not think in syndicalist terms despite their expressed goals, but the comparative moderation of strike demands at least suggests a high probability.

However, an examination of the political goals of French strikes is not the most important way to compare syndicalists' and workers' intentions. It is easy to show that, while syndicalists continued to hope for an ultimate general strike, workers shied away from remote strike demands, whether these were in some way political or simply directed toward general labor solidarity. Syndicalists realized this, so they attempted only a few such strikes. They turned increasingly to the guidance of ordinary strikes, partly to train workers in combat and class consciousness and partly because as union leaders they could not avoid this role. In this role, they distinguished themselves from reformist leaders in France and elsewhere by encouraging relatively exaggerated demands. Often they sought an eight-hour day instead of a nine-hour day, or a 25% instead of a 10% wage increase. Hence, to test the relevance of syndicalist leadership in practice, we must try to determine the extent to which French workers were interested or could be persuaded to be interested in agitation for substantial material gains. In fact, syndicalist success in this area too was slight and usually ephemeral.

Increasingly, as the period wore on, syndicalists encouraged their charges to press for solid gains instead of relatively ephemeral pay increases: hence they worked for improvements in hours of work and for written agreements covering all sorts of working conditions. Workers did respond to this approach, the closest to visible and realizable material gains. But the response was incomplete; and, ironically, the syndicalists who urged this approach were behaving no differently than reformist labor leaders in France and elsewhere. Because of the weakness of syndicalist goals and organization, French workers resisted the pressure to turn away from strikes over minor wage issues and personal questions more fully and successfully than those in any other industrial country.

We are not, then, trying merely to test the relevance of syndicalism's theoretical aims to the French strike movement. Syndicalist trade unions tried gradually to radicalize their members, and finally, almost in desperation, they began to concentrate on simply trying to obtain more durable results from strikes. In all these efforts syndicalists acted on a belief in the possibility of progress through collective action. French workers were awakening only slowly and unevenly to such a notion. This is really the principal point to investigate.

Political Goals and Solidarity

Students of French labor have long noted the workers' fear of the long-range aims of syndicalism as one reason for the somewhat slow growth of union membership in France and for the fact that only about half of the French unions were in the C.G.T. In strikes, workers often avoided appeals to outside agitators lest they do more harm than good, and many more, though seeking tactical guidance from any quarter, were frightened by the speeches outsiders made. Ribbon weavers in Saint-Étienne in 1900 beat up a speaker who had urged acceptance of revolutionary ideas. Only rarely could more than a small minority be won over, and often syndicalist speeches led to defections that destroyed a strike. This prompted some syndicalists to doubt the efficacy of strike activity; others, still convinced of its ultimate educational value, moderated their speeches as well as their tactics in the hope that a strong labor movement could be developed. Thus, Griffuelhes and his colleagues avoided any mention of politics or religion among the vigorous but Catholic, conservative leatherworkers in Mazamet.[1]

Many workers who listened to syndicalist speeches and were moved at least by the excitement of a strike carried anarchist or syndicalist banners in demonstrations. This was commonly the case in the rare but important metallurgical strikes, such as the one at Le Creusot in 1900. But it is impossible to believe that many workers maintained their exalted mood or understood clearly what syndicalism meant. Some Le Creusot workers, it is true, left town after their strike because of their rage at the company, though most of the approximately two thousand exiles were driven out by their employer. Many of them went to Lorraine, where in the 1905 strike they behaved conservatively, chastened by their early experience. Perhaps they still harbored revolutionary thoughts, but if so they kept them rigorously private. As to the majority of workers who stayed at Le Creusot, they accepted a company union, which gave them a real but limited voice over working conditions, with every appearance of contentment, though of course under great pressure from the company to do so. In other words, workers seldom displayed a durable commitment to slogans and symbols that briefly appealed to them in particularly bitter strikes over economic issues.

Equally important, French workers do not seem to have believed that strikes explicitly for abstract or political purposes were appropriate. The response to calls for observance of May Day as a demonstration of labor's solidarity was usually limited, though syndicalist as well as socialist leaders urged workers to take the day off each year. Precise figures are impossible here, but it seems clear that fewer French than German workers observed May Day, despite the fact that French employers were less likely than German to punish their workers for such observance. Typically, after 1900, French participants were workers who were excited by a campaign or an issue in their own local industry; the unemployed; state workers; and a few others who were given full freedom to take the day off. The result was rarely a massive display. Paris led the way of course, though usually the percentage of participation was low. Saint-Étienne also figured prominently, and syndicalists were admittedly strong in the city: employers there allowed workers to take the day off if they chose. Finally workers in cities with big military arsenals, whose employer was the government, often joined the May Day effort. But far more workers rarely participated, even those who, like the miners, were active in the strike movement as a whole. In 1913, 5,993 of 70,000 workers around Valenciennes took May Day off. Of these 3,800 were metallurgical workers—but they constituted only a tenth of the region's total in this industry. Obviously more workers than this felt solidarity with some aspect of the labor movement, but a walk-out, even for a day, was too risky and expensive to be used for an essentially symbolic goal.[2]

A few big strikes had vague political overtones which syndicalists encouraged. Railroad workers in 1910, particularly in Paris, were angry at the government over inadequate pension laws and then over Briand's mobilization of their ranks; in strike meetings, a few workers suggested demonstrations against the government, but were dissuaded by the lack of interest of their fellows and their leaders' fear that they would be arrested. Yet the syndicalist press had promoted a rail strike as a direct attack on the state. The C.G.T. sponsored a one-day nation-wide strike against war on December 10, 1912. It claimed that 600,000 workers heeded the call, but this seems doubtful. Only a handful of miners struck. In Marseilles, about 500 metallurgical and construction workers walked off their jobs. In France as a whole, only arsenal and shipbuilding workers seem to have been widely drawn to the movement. It is unlikely that more than 50,000 workers actually left their jobs for the day. The strike was a failure. And this was the only effort of the kind. French workers ultimately became adept at strikes to embarrass the state, but in this period when syndicalists so clearly stressed the importance of the strike as an antigovernment weapon they did not accept any kind of political implications in their strikes. Too many workers were politically apathetic or divided; too many, including most socialists, saw the government as a potential if limited friend in industrial conflict.[3]

Only three groups of workers struck even for specific legislation. In 1903 Parisian bakers and barbers (who were syndicalist-led) resumed a campaign to win legal abolition of private employment agencies. Yet the resulting strikes were small; in Paris, for example, only 189 of 5,500 food workers joined in.[4] Only miners and merchant seamen, whose strike activities revealed unusual sophistication in most respects, made important efforts to influence legislation. The seamen and the northern miners were not led by syndicalists, though the miners elsewhere were; but the point is not significant since strikes for reform legislation were inconsistent with syndicalist theory anyway. In 1907 about a quarter of the merchant seamen in Marseilles struck for higher pensions, while all of the major miners' strikes shortly before the war were designed to press parliament on legislation covering pensions and hours of work. Syndicalist leaders were, admittedly, trying to discredit the government by persuading the miners to attack existing laws and proposals; but the miners themselves struck, not against the government, but for a positive gain that they cherished as basic to the "security, dignity, and happiness of our old age."[5] The March 1914 strike to force parliament to improve the recently passed law won at least 50% participation in most of the basins in France.

Generally, however, legislative issues of this sort aroused little interest, at least from a syndicalist standpoint. C.G.T. meetings against the voluntary pension law, held in 1910 and 1911, stressed that dues were too high and pensions too low; and some workers were annoyed about new withholdings. In most cities, however, the meetings drew only a few hundred workers; 1,200 attended in Fougères, for example, but only 400 in Marseilles. And there were no strikes directly over this issue.[6]

Few strikes, then, revealed much interest in the political process. Striking workers at most complained to government officials about the execution of existing laws, but they sought administrative adjustment and not positive, legal change. Syndicalism may have played a role in this neglect of politics, because its advocates among the most vigorous union leaders could not easily bring themselves to guide workers toward limited political demands—another case where syndicalism's impact in France was largely negative, delaying the development of greater sophistication among workers rather than forming positive characteristics. What was equally important, syndicalism delayed the formation of strong national unions, which were a precondition for pressure on the legislature. Yet even this negative impact must not be pressed too far. Most French union members did not ignore politics altogether; they at least voted. Their reluctance to employ strikes to press legislative demands was typical of the experience of most industrial countries: British miners, for example, learned to use strikes to win government action only in 1912. Once groups of French workers began to turn in this direction, syndicalist leaders had to follow, as in the case of the miners. And the whole logic of the strike movement as a means of obtaining durable gains ultimately prompted syndicalists to press the workers to seek reforms from the government, though, as we have seen, their effort often met with indifferent success. After 1910 syndicalist leaders were urging social legislation with the best of the reformist stalwarts, though with different rhetoric. Here is, in fact, a typical pattern. Workers had been largely content with syndicalist urgings, in this instance to play down the possibility of using strikes to win reforms from parliament, but for their own reasons. Nonsyndicalist workers were not noticeably different from apparently syndicalist workers in this regard. Experience taught syndicalist leaders to alter their advice, but workers were not quick to change their own minds. Where there was no overwhelming grievance about suffrage rights, as was the case in France, strikes and politics were very slow to mix. Syndicalism had little to do with this fact.

Finally, even general solidarity strikes were rare in France—much rarer than in Britain or Germany. Unless workers had demands of their own or were intensely aware of unfair repression, it was hard to get them out for such strikes; and the loose organization of French unions prevented rapid correction of this attitude. French printers made a common sentiment explicit. Despite intensive propaganda, they voted 6,333 to 1,196 against joining a solidarity strike over police brutality towards quarry workers in Draveil in 1908. Workers that were more occasionally employed or altogether unemployed were more open to the excitement of a solidarity strike, particularly of course in Paris. Many construction workers in Le Havre protested the assassination of a union leader in 1910. But again, more opportunities for a sympathy strike were ignored than taken up. Miners even in the syndicalist-led center could not be roused to express solidarity with their comrades in Montceau in 1901; only handfuls of workers, all from the building trades, heeded sympathy-strike calls in 1909 for postal employees, and in 1910 for the railroads. A sympathy strike even by workers in a different branch of the same company occurred only once or twice.[7] Demonstrations of solidarity were of course more common. We need not ignore the well-known marches of thousands of Parisian workers in behalf of victims of police repression in 1908 and 1909. It is worthy of note that so few workers assumed the greater burden of a strike for such a cause. The French efforts were mild in comparison with the violence of the solidarity protest in Berlin-Moabit in 1909 and with the frequency of solidarity movements in Britain after 1910. There is no instance in any industry in France before World War I of workers taking up the cause of a person outside their area who seemed to have been unfairly treated, as was so common among railroad workers and others in Britain in 1912 and 1913. In this matter also, workers were not generally interested in the sort of strikes syndicalists wanted. If the syndicalists produced any distinctive patterns in France in this period it was only by indirection and against their own intent: they lacked the solid union organizations to encourage broader boycotts, which were slow to develop in other industrial countries as well.[8]

Scope of Material Demands

Some French workers were receptive to the syndicalist tendency to push for exaggerated demands in strikes in order to win major gains for workers and to teach them the need for a frontal attack on recalcitrant employers and the capitalist system. The most general effort in this direction was the great eight-hour-day strike of 1906, which the C.G.T. carefully prepared. Most workers had a ten-hour day, so that the eight-hour demand was truly radical. For this reason the reformist unions stayed away from the effort; the printers' federation, most notably, struck separately for a nine-hour day, though its Parisian branch rebelled and tried for eight. Between 1904 and 1906, the movement was prepared by countless lectures, pamphlets, and posters; the Paris metallurgical union alone sponsored 250 speeches. And the movement caught on. On May 1, 1906, there were 285 strikes, involving 202,507 workers and affecting 12,585 companies. Parisian workers, particularly in the building trades and metal industries, provided most of the impetus to the movement. Most of the metalworkers in the Saint-Étienne area also struck, and agitation touched many other cities.[9]

Here is proof that at least a minority of workers could be drawn to a radical strike. The importance of the strike in Paris shows once again real syndicalist strength in the capital. But a few qualifications must be added, aside from the fact that this is the only major success the C.G.T.

had in a radical strike. Many Parisian workers, particularly mechanics, realized from the start that the eight-hour demand was unrealistic and despite the directive from their union strove only for Saturday afternoon off; other groups quickly turned to this demand when it soon became clear that the eight-hour day could not be attained. Large numbers of construction workers were found, to the despair of their leaders, actually asking for a pay raise instead of shorter hours. Demands for the eight-hour day were only occasionally heard after this great and abortive effort. A few construction strikes in Paris repeated the demand, while dock workers, who were not syndicalist-led, alone tried consistently to achieve the goal, with a recurrent slogan of "8 hours, 6 francs." In the period as a whole, there were fewer strikes for eight hours than occurred in Germany. German metal and construction workers were notably more vigorous and successful in this demand than their French counterparts.[10] The 1906 strike obviously cannot be dismissed, but equally obviously it was exceptional. Many more strikers resisted excessive demands, like the northern miners who, despite huge grievances and the highest strike rate in France, rejected the small syndicalist union's catchy slogan of "8 hours, 8 francs" for fear that they would compromise a reduction in hours by excessive demands and because, after 1906, many of them were satisfied with their rising money wages anyway.[11]

The point is that French workers as a whole, despite their impressive strike activity, sought only limited and often traditional goals before World War I. They frequently disappointed the positive hopes of their leaders, and this was true in reformist unions as well as in syndicalist groups. The ceramic workers' federation noted: "A large part of the working class, the most miserable part, seem to be resigned to misery, because they don't know the reasons for it. They endure the fact and are ignorant of the causes." [12] The poorest segment of the labor force rarely protested at all; there was nothing, in France, to compare to the awakening of female and rural manufacturing workers in Britain after 1910. The vast majority of French workers never struck during this period. If the average miner struck over three times between 1899 and 1913, the average skilled construction worker struck only 1.3 times (despite the importance of syndicalism in this group); and these were the only large industrial categories in which the number of strikers between 1899 and 1914 exceeded the number of workers in the industry. Huge industries like textiles, despite numerous strikes in certain centers, were normally quiet over most of France. These facts in no way eliminate the possibility that syndicalism was the vehicle of the active minority of workers;

more important for our purposes is the modest character of most actual strike demands.

The nature of workers' goals emerged most clearly in strikes over wage questions, which constituted 63% of all strikes in the period. Like all major strike goals, wage demands covered a variety of actual grievances; they were, also, the easiest type of demand to win. But in this period, wage demands predominated not because workers had rising expectations but because they had to defend levels they had already achieved. Syndicalists, who worked for positive gains, had little to do with this effort and were often disgusted by it.

Broadly speaking, French strike rates conformed to the cycles of the economy, dropping when the economy declined and rising when prosperity returned. Most workers realized that they had little chance of winning a strike in a slump; but we cannot say that they struck in this period to gain a larger stake in the general prosperity. Moreover, the relationship between strikes and economic conditions is incomplete. In the recession year of 1902 there was a rise in the strike rate as workers sought to protest bad conditions. Strikes declined over the preceding year in 1905, 1911, and 1913, despite the fact that each of these years was increasingly prosperous. Further, the industries and regions most rapidly advancing in prosperity and benefiting from the fullest employment were not the leaders in protest activity. The east of France, which was gaining rapidly in cotton and particularly metallurgical production, was not a center for strikes. Compared to the metallurgical industry, the textile industry lagged badly throughout the period, yet it produced far more protest (so much, in terms of numbers of strikes, that it contributed disproportionately to the overall pattern of the French strike movement). And textile strikes often increased during the years of economic difficulty for the industry, which were more frequent than general national recessions. For example, 1904 was a bad year for cotton and wool despite national prosperity; unemployment was high. Yet strikes multiplied rapidly. In 1907, a good year even for textiles, the weavers in Flers de l'Orne suffered from a severe local slump; and because of this they instituted the only elaborate protest they conducted during the whole period. Graulhet leather-dressers, who were not inexperienced in the labor movement, struck frequently in 1907 despite the fact that over half of them were unemployed.[13] The common and facile assumption that economic trends closely determine strike rates needs modification for this period, as well as the assumption that workers carefully awaited a boom in order to win unprecedented earnings.

Many workers were simply not dissatisfied with their wages in normal times. Union officials often lamented the willingness of construction workers to enjoy their summer pay without a thought for the winter of unemployment. Union campaigns to induce highly organized workers to agitate for a raise often met widespread indifference, particularly after 1911 when real wages had stopped falling. Contemporary surveys indicated that workers had some desire for more money to spend on food and perhaps on clothing and entertainment, but less interest in improving their housing or furniture or medical care. Their unwillingness to change their spending habits significantly was the basis of their usual indifference to collective efforts to raise their income above existing levels.[14]

A desire for positive gains did spread during the prewar years. It often occurred in rather gradual stages, but it was unquestionably a measure of growing sophistication. Most important, it spread widely among younger workers, and the strike movement was not the only evidence of this. In many skilled occupations there were reports of anxiety among the young to earn quickly, at the expense of thorough or traditional training, and to abandon the trades of their fathers when the gains did not seem large enough. This development doubtless set the stage for the more aggressive strike action after World War I, but it had not by 1914 characterized French agitation generally.[15]

According to the official statistics, the defensive wage demand, the protest against a reduction in pay, constituted less than a tenth of all wage demands in strikes, and it declined rather steadily during the period itself. The statistics are accurate only in the most literal sense of indicating when workers walked out at the announcement of a reduction. They reveal but a small fraction of the cases in which worker dissatisfaction was based on a desire to restore previous salary levels. The workers' most common argument in asking for a pay raise stressed the need to maintain or restore the usual standard of living. Admittedly, this argument was calculated to win public sympathy by appealing to what most people (even some employers) thought justified a wage increase, but it reflected worker attitudes as well.

The first strike of cloth designers in Nantes occurred in 1906. Their pay had been cut in 1903, and then a period of unemployment ensued during which they were too sensible to strike. But when work picked up in 1905, they expected a raise and struck when they did not receive one; yet they asked only for a restoration of pre-1903 levels. In 1907 workers in a Vosges textile plant struck for a raise to compensate for a new system of pay that maintained the previous daily rate but no longer covered days off; workers noted that a 5% raise would simply restore a wage level that had long been common in the area. The first nation-wide miners' strike, in 1902, occurred because of a general reduction in bonuses; the miners asked for a raise, but only to make up for their lost bonus. There is no need to belabor the point. A large number of strikes that apparently sought higher wage rates in reality were defending accustomed levels. Sometimes, to be sure, the rate that was defended had been a raise a few years before; French workers had obviously improved their standards of living in the preceding decades, but they still had not collectively displayed a commitment to steady progress in the future.[16]

Demands for higher wages covered a variety of effective reductions in pay. Workers protested new withholdings, particularly for pensions, in a few strikes. Strikes for a raise to compensate for a period of unemployment were more important; again, the purpose was to maintain accustomed standards. The first big Fougères strike, in 1906–1907, invoked the massive unemployment earlier in 1906 as its principal argument for a raise. More generally, wage demands were especially common in industries with fluctuating employment, such as construction work, and often the first major strike resulted from an unusually severe period of unemployment. This sometimes taught the strikers that further, positive raises could be sought, but the first effort was typically defensive.[17]

Directly defensive strikes occurred also to compensate for a decline in the hours of work and a resulting decline in pay. In September 1907, Parisian masons, particularly the masons' aides, asked for the maintenance of their nine-hours' pay despite the recent introduction of an eight-hour day. Only in later years did large groups of Parisian masons ask for positive increases in their pay. The great rail strike of 1910 began in the Chapelle-Saint Denis depot when track-maintenance workers asked for a raise to replace the cessation of overtime. Series of strikes in the textile industry occurred between 1900 and 1904 to win a raise sufficient to maintain existing pay despite the reduction of hours of work by law. A smaller number of strikes occurred in some crafts as a result of the legal provision of a weekly day off.[18]

A large number of apparently progressive strikes after 1903 sought an increase in pay to compensate for the rise in prices. French workers were unusually quick to realize that inflation was occurring. This was probably because they had lower real wages and so less margin than British workers and fewer nonmonetary resources, like gardens and livestock, than German and Belgian workers. Their persistent emphasis on wage demands reflects an outlook that was especially sensitive to inflation. In any case, despite the fact that their inflation was less severe, French workers perceived it much more quickly than British workers before the war. French housewives, who seldom found any appeal in syndicalism, led in the adoption of this new issue. Better budget-keepers than the British, they could soon report that prices were rising; it seems to have taken years for some British women to tell their husbands what was happening, and so strike demands based on price-rises were almost a decade behind the actual inflation.[19] Certainly France was the only industrial country to experience market riots by women during the prewar years. The riots vividly recall traditional reactions to price increases in food, again suggesting some continuities in protest that no new labor doctrine could easily displace.

From about 1906 onward, striking workers began to claim that their pay was inadequate because of price increases. Their claims antedated syndicalist campaigns against "la vie chère" by several years. Their argument was often a simple one, as in the case of the paper workers who said that a raise was "indispensable just to allow us to live." [20] Masons in Béziers noted in 1911 that their pay had not changed since 1895 but that the cost of wine (which they consumed at the rate of two liters a day) had risen 25%. The reasoning was clear, as the Marseilles maritime union noted in 1912: "If food prices rise in a certain proportion, wages must follow in the same proportion." [21] And these claims persisted until the war, even though the pressure on real wages probably lightened, for many workers were still trying to make good earlier losses. Bakers in the Seine-et-Oise expressed the common sentiment in 1913: "For fifteen years everything has risen at a phenomenal rate and our pay hasn't changed . . ." [22]

In France and in other countries, the persistent inflation of these years was instrumental in developing a desire for improvements in pay. Though strikes on this issue were at first defensive, to maintain existing standards, they accustomed many workers to the idea of asking for higher real wages. However, this conversion was still incomplete by 1914. The leveling off of the strike rate after 1910 indicated, among other things, that many workers remained content so long as real wages did not fall.

Other types of wage demands were, similarly, transitional between a desire to maintain traditional levels and a real demand for improvement. Many workers sought a raise to compensate for an increase in the difficulty or pace of work or for work on new machines. Some innovations led to lower pay, as when employers cut piece rates more than was necessary to compensate for the greater productivity of machines. But here again, change could lead workers from a defensive reaction to a demand for positive gains. Printers who struck frequently over rates for work on compositor machines insisted on higher pay than ever before. The rapid changes in the pace and methods of work in the years before the war persuaded them and other workers of the desirability of striking for more money.[23]

Still another common inducement to seek higher real wages was the increasing realization that wages varied greatly for the same job. Very often workers asked simply that they be given what their fellows were getting, and of course the unions encouraged efforts to generalize the highest level of existing pay. The basic sentiment was simple, as Lille weavers noted: "We want Pierre, Paul or Jacques to be paid the same price for the same work."[24] Another existing standard was frequently invoked, especially by construction workers. Many cities had "series prices," essentially recommended wage rates for most types of construction work, often drawn up several decades before and rarely applied, and public contractors included wage rates in their bids for contracts, again without honoring them in practice. The first generalized strikes among Parisian construction workers cited the 1882 series price list as the major justification for wage demands. And in Paris and elsewhere, construction strike movements commonly began on public projects, where contractors' failures to live up to their own wage lists provided an obvious goal for demands, and then spread more slowly to private sites where the wages of public-works employees were also claimed.[25] Here again, many workers could not at first strike for an abstract raise. They had to have an existing standard, not just to use for public argument but to convince themselves that their effort had justification in precedent. Once they grew used to the notion, however, some of them could dispense with the reference. By 1908 Parisian construction workers were agitating for unprecedented raises, well beyond the city series levels.[26]

In general, then, the massive increase in strike activity resulted from growing difficulties in maintaining existing standards more than from rising expectations, though there was an evolution toward greater sophistication in wage demands. The same absence of a generally progressive mentality also characterized other strike demands, as we shall see. This is why syndicalist efforts to push workers toward relatively sweeping material goals were largely ignored and also why most workers who called in a syndicalist leader to help them with a strike did so for purely tactical purposes, remaining uninterested in the collective progress he would urge or not convinced that it was possible.

The relationship between a belief in material progress and participation in a radical movement like syndicalism is a complex one. In this period, French textile workers, among the most purely defensive in their wage demands, were the main working-class constituents of the most revolutionary wing of the socialist movement. We can assume, then, that modest immediate demands were compatible with, possibly encouraged by, belief in a future utopia. Syndicalism, for all that it promised a golden future, could not fill this role as well as socialism. Its weapon was the strike; it did not wait for a general strike but became increasingly involved with limited efforts; strikes made no sense without some achievable goals; and with this we return to the limited expectations of most workers. Syndicalist leaders, like union leaders in most countries except perhaps Britain, faced a more prosaic task than the inculcation of their doctrine. They had to cut through the defensive mentality of their charges to encourage a positive strike movement. Their doctrine was important in sustaining them in this difficult effort, but it had little direct relevance to their constituents.

Syndicalists helped some workers develop an idea of effective progress in material standards, but there is no evidence that they were more successful than reformist leaders. Syndicalists, after all, approached the problem with divided minds. They wanted the workers to ask for significant gains, but they also preached the coming revolution. Even workers who paid little attention to the revolutionary promptings might have been somewhat distracted from the other lesson. In contrast, reformists like the printers' or northern miners' leaders tried to teach the possibility of significant if gradual progress more single-mindedly, and their charges led France in solidly progressive strikes.

Differences in Expectation

There were, in fact, great differences within the labor force in the nature of wage demands. The defensive character of the average *strike* was due above all to the frequency of efforts by textile workers and other traditionalist elements. The average *striker* is harder to characterize, particularly because of the size of many mining strikes. In general, two types of workers developed progressive pay demands. Unskilled workers wanted a great deal right away. Their expectations were rarely due to syndicalism; near misery and a realization of how far they lagged behind

other workers were the real causes. But syndicalism could have appealed
to these workers and increased their demands. Only in one major case,
however, did it really do so and then without producing particularly
distinctive or durable results. Miners and craftsmen raised more limited
demands, but they wanted progressive improvement or came to want it.
Some of them were in syndicalist unions, some were not. The point is
that syndicalism did not cause or even noticeably heighten these crucial
differences in the French labor force. The differences stemmed rather
from differences in traditions and the nature of the work and could be
found in all the industrial countries. Unions encouraged the rising expectation of some groups, but it did not matter much if they were syndicalist or not. Syndicalism helped rouse new demands but so did other
doctrines, or unions with no doctrines at all. It is hard, then, to attribute
any distinctive importance to syndicalist efforts to shape the strike movement.

One of the most important developments in French labor in this period
was the awakening of unskilled workers, notably dockers and construction laborers (*terrassiers*). Their awakening was often as vigorous as
it was sudden, and their demands in wages and other matters were almost limitless. These workers, oppressed by low pay and frequent unemployment, did not justify their demands by the standards of the
past. Sometimes they argued for a wage increase because their jobs
were too hard. Le Havre dockers unloading saltpeter in 1910, because
their loads were too heavy, suddenly struck with a demand for a 25%
raise. Others simply cited their misery; a strike of quarry workers in the
Loire in 1902 won a raise of almost 25%, to three and a quarter francs a
day, on this basis. Demands for reduced hours by unskilled workers were
far-reaching too. Dockers often insisted on eight hours as a means of
curtailing unemployment (which often rose to 30% of the labor force
in bad seasons), while carters sought 20% shorter hours because their cur-
rent levels of fourteen or fifteen hours a day were, they suddenly realized, unendurable.[27]

Here, then, were groups of workers with large demands. They had
little previous experience in strikes and thus little sense of what was
realistic. They struck out of genuine misery and a knowledge that other
types of workers enjoyed far better conditions than theirs. Potentially, the
unskilled workers were open to syndicalism, as an expression of their
radical discontent and desire to strike. In some cases, syndicalist leaders
reached them. In Paris, syndicalists played a significant role in the agitation of the unskilled, particularly in the construction industry but also

among railroad maintenance men. By 1908 the C.G.T. was also sending leaders to organize quarry workers in nearby departments, especially the Seine-et-Oise, and to guide a few strikes elsewhere (notably those of railroad maintenance men in southwestern France and of construction laborers in Aix-en-Provence). But there is little sign that syndicalism converted many of these workers for any extended period of time, and the initial burst of strikes by the unskilled often set developments in motion that changed the character of strike demands. And though syndicalist speakers addressed dockers frequently, the main dockers' and seamen's unions were not syndicalist. In Marseilles, particularly, dockers roused themselves without external help (though the socialist mayor provided some guidance); they did not need imported doctrines. Syndicalists lost valuable potential support in failing to win the dockers.

The situation in the Parisian construction industry is the only case where the role of syndicalism among the unskilled needs serious assessment and in fact it illustrates the difficulty of treating syndicalism as a basic force. Was syndicalism a cause of the agitation or was it simply present, providing organizational guidance but little real inspiration? From 1906 to 1909 or 1910, construction workers in Paris, mainly unskilled laborers and skilled masons, were in almost constant turmoil, led by the syndicalist building trades' federation. The 1906 strike for an eight-hour day had set things off. It followed several years of unemployment and sinking wages; and the construction of the Paris metro, because it provided numerous but also unusually difficult jobs, served as an obvious spur. Strikes and slowdowns were endemic, and, encouraged by their leaders, workers demanded unprecedentedly high wages and short hours. Here, in the center of syndicalist strength, is the most genuine link between syndicalism and extensive, persistent agitation in the period. We cannot know, of course, how many of the strikers accepted or even understood syndicalist doctrines, but surely they were touched by them.

There are two problems, however, in associating syndicalism with even these workers as a basic or enduring force. First, similar risings of the unskilled occurred in many places without significant syndicalist involvement. Marseilles dockers showed comparable fervor in their salad years, 1900–1904. During the very years of the Paris unrest, 1906–1909, Berlin construction workers displayed an almost identical surge of excitement. In 1906, against the advice of their union, they struck for an eight-hour day. The next year they rejected a raise that their union urged them to accept and struck again. Numerous more limited strikes, frequent attacks on the more timid workers, indeed the whole range of

"Parisian" symptoms prevailed for more than two years. And the causes involved were the same, if syndicalism is omitted: rising employment after several years of stagnation combined with the special spur of public works in a growing capital city.[28] It is more appropriate to view the Paris strikes as a common early manifestation of a new assertiveness of the unskilled than as a syndicalist development. Moreover, all the extensive risings of the unskilled in syndicalist Paris as elsewhere, were quickly cut off. Employers, taken by surprise at first, rallied within a few years, forming new defensive associations and bringing in some new workers. Strikes in Paris after 1909, as in Berlin or Marseilles, had to be conducted more calmly and with more limited demands. At the same time, workers, having won extensive gains, were no longer so acutely discontent.

Many other groups of workers wanted positive improvements in their conditions. In a few professions, relatively well-paid workers argued for better wages as a share in the rising prosperity of their industry. Metallurgical workers in Pamiers struck in 1906, when they learned that their company had augmented its capital by a million and a half francs, though they asked only for a restoration of pre-1902 wage levels. Construction workers often sought to profit from a boom in their industry; new public-works projects prompted Saint-Malo workers to claim that "we must profit from these millions to be gained in the works under contract, to raise our pay." [29] Workers often cited inflated profit margins on such projects as well. But coal miners, even more than construction workers, wanted positive improvements based on rising prices of coal. Even in 1898 the Loire miners' union argued for its wage demand "on grounds that the miners are one of the factors in production and that, as such, they should in a certain measure benefit from the increased price of their products." [30]

These workers had an effective sense of progress that French labor as a whole lacked. This sense undoubtedly spread during the period. Glove workers in Milhau conducted several major strikes between 1900 and 1913, largely on wage issues. Their first strikes were against wage reductions and price increases; they did not ask for absolute improvements. But in 1913, spurred by a new American tariff that brought higher prices for gloves, they broke a contract and struck for a substantial raise, justifying their demand in part as a desire for their "normal and constant raise." [31]

Most of the "progressive" workers did not seek huge gains, however. We have seen that northern miners rejected syndicalist slogans; miners around Saint-Étienne, syndicalist-led, were even more moderate in their actual demands. Skilled construction workers in the provinces worked for piecemeal gains. In 1913 the La Rochelle construction workers' union tried to persuade its members to strike for a raise to share in the building boom of that year; but it aroused no interest, for workers were pleased at their high rates of employment, which they did not want to jeopardize in a risky strike. Finally, some of the most progressive workers, particularly the miners, benefited from a rise in real wages in the period. They had no need to strike for great sums in terms of their expectations, and in fact strikes over wage issues occurred 15%–30% less frequently in their industries than in the nation as a whole.[32] If in the excitement of a strike the most progressive workers occasionally asked for a big raise, even bigger than a syndicalist leader had suggested, they were almost always ready to accept much less, and few strikes were prolonged because workers rejected a moderate wage offer.

With one possible exception, no major group of French workers under syndicalist leadership went farther or faster in progressive wage demands than its counterparts in other industrial countries where syndicalism played no role. Skilled construction and metalworkers asked for no more than the German or British did, perhaps less in fact, because their leaders paid less consistent attention to bread-and-butter demands and because the weakness of their union organizations inhibited them. Only leather dressers (syndicalist-led, though decidedly not syndicalist) broke the pattern at all by their firm desire for higher pay. Again, the development of new material expectations was not really under syndicalist control, so the leading issues in strikes escaped the movement.

Reshaping Strike Demands

Because of their lack of control over wage demands and because of the limits on these demands and their results, syndicalists tried increasingly to induce workers to strive for something more than the maintenance or even the improvement of wages. Like labor leaders in most countries, they learned that wage gains could be ephemeral. Employers cut them back at the earliest opportunity, and in industries like mining and metals where wages were kept secret and individuals earned variable amounts on a piece rate it was difficult to tell what actual pay levels were. Hence syndicalists, like labor leaders everywhere, began to urge written agreements. In this they encountered little resistance, and one of their greatest contributions to labor relations in France was their encouragement of collective bargaining. Some workers resisted of course. Some may have learned from early syndicalists that written agreements with employers were traps and then have resisted later syndicalist promptings to sign such agreements. But most resistance came from workers who felt that the issue was too abstract or were offended by the idea of written, equalized wage rates, and resistance was no greater than in other industrial countries. However, demands for written agreements spread. Miners had long been aware of their importance. Textile, leather, and construction workers asked for written rates and received them with growing frequency. By 1912, merchant seamen and dockers were agitating for national rates.[33] Again, syndicalism did not lead to distinctive behavior, for written agreements spread at least as widely in nonsyndicalist as in syndicalist unions and areas. But here, at least, syndicalists advocated what the situation demanded and what workers wanted, so they could claim a success. Or rather, they could have claimed a success had they not been syndicalists and therefore more than a little embarrassed by one of their real achievements.

In addition to written agreements and to meet the problem of inadequate or impermanent wage gains, syndicalist union leaders pressed for agitation for shorter hours and safer working conditions. In this, too, they were advocating what socialists and reformists advocated. To judge the syndicalists' success in inducing workers to strike for lower hours is not, then, a distinctive test of syndicalism. But it is important to note that French workers were probably more resistant to these inducements than workers elsewhere because of their preoccupation with defending their wage levels. Again, the influence of syndicalists proved inadequate to overcome the workers' self-conceived interests. In this matter as in so many others, the syndicalists' chief contribution to the enduring character of French labor was negative; their unions and bureaucracy were too weak to handle the difficult task of altering workers' attitudes. To be sure, 24% of French strikes from 1899 to 1913 stressed demands relating to the conditions of work; 15% sought a change, usually a reduction, in the hours of work. Compared to other national strike percentages, however, these figures are rather low. The French working day, though longer than the British, seldom exceeded ten hours; for many workers, in industries such as textiles where women were involved, it was reduced to ten hours by law between 1900 and 1904. Most workers were not actively dissatisfied with their hours of work or at any rate believed that other matters were more important. For them to demand a reduction of hours meant a positive improvement in conditions that were already endurable, and as we have seen an effective sense of the possibility of progress had not widely developed.

In fact, the groups that most frequently pushed for a reduction in hours did so either out of unusual hardship or to compensate for some other change in their conditions. In the first category were barbers and bakers, who often worked sixteen hours a day every day of the week, and many carters, tram workers, and seamen; about a quarter of their strikes concerned a reduction of hours or a weekly day off. The very high incidence of strikes by printers to reduce hours was primarily motivated by the increasing mechanization of their trade. They wanted shorter hours because the pace of work was rising and above all to protect their jobs. Dockers also saw curtailed hours principally as a means to cut unemployment. And many metalworkers reacted against efforts to increase their pace of work, though as a group they did not seek lower hours with unusual frequency.[34]

Syndicalist leaders complained time and time again that their efforts to direct agitation toward a reduction of hours were ignored. In a common pattern, the leader of Graulhet leatherworkers pushed for a strike for a nine-hour day in 1910, only to find that his followers just wanted a twenty-five-centime raise. Despite the great success of the C.G.T. eight-hour-day campaign in 1906, the workers' interest soon lagged. In the period as a whole, strikes over questions of hours declined; in 1913 only 9% of all strikes involved this issue. The later, extensive C.G.T. campaign for a five-and-a-half-day week, the "English week," met widespread indifference. Even the sophisticated miners, who were interested in lower hours in many cases, often rebelled against their leaders. Union efforts to persuade miners to protest overtime work, the "longues coupes," or simply to avoid the work when management allowed them to, frequently failed. Employers often pressed miners to work overtime, but workers were also influenced by their desire for extra earnings and their traditional practice of working overtime in certain periods. Construction workers were the despair of syndicalist leaders in this regard. When faced with a choice between shorter hours and a pay raise they almost always took the latter. Masons in Saint-Malo in 1911 believed that it was wrong to ask, as their union suggested, for a nine-hour day as well as a ten-centime raise per hour. Many construction workers believed they had plenty of rest in the winter. Gradually they saw the utility in striking for shorter hours, but mainly as a means of earning more money. Rarely did they cut their time at work if they won a reduction through a strike; they preferred to enjoy overtime rates for their final hour on the job.[35]

This is not to say, of course, that demands for shorter hours were unimportant, and many workers struck over this issue. The campaign for the "English week" caused a general textile strike in Saint-Quentin and appealed to many metalworkers; in 1913 a number of automobile workers conducted their first strikes over this issue. But many workers ignored such campaigns and many who struck for shorter hours ignored the reasoning behind the syndicalist programs. The syndicalists, like labor leaders generally, wanted workers to strike for reduced hours chiefly to gain more leisure, though they did not ignore other benefits such as a higher rate of employment. They wanted workers to have time to improve their family life, to acquire more culture, and more knowledge about society. Doubtless many workers approved of these purposes, but it is not clear that many thought they were feasible goals in strikes. Strike demands that were not simply phrased in formulas prepared by a union seldom mentioned leisure as the main issue; they stressed the need to reduce unemployment or to compensate for mechanization. At most, workers were anxious to reduce the hours of women. Fougères shoe workers in 1913 asked for an "English week" but made it clear that they were particularly concerned about giving the women a half day to do shopping and housework.[36] Women in many places showed this concern; silk spinners in the Gard complained that "we're prisoners in the shop from Monday morning to Saturday night"[37]—but women were not likely to join unions or to strike.

The syndicalists' role in shaping strike goals consisted chiefly of nudging workers in directions the workers were already moving and in advocating what moderate unions advocated. It is hard to see that French strike goals would have been much different without the presence of syndicalism. Yet we must shift gears for a moment, for there is a large category of demands still untouched. Syndicalists did not directly urge these demands; but the demands may nonetheless denote a distinctively French characteristic relevant to syndicalism and a level of worker anger that contributed to syndicalism and was encouraged by it in turn.

Personal Issues and Employer Relations

Twenty-five percent of all strikes in the prewar years involved demands that workers be hired or fired or that foremen or managers be retained or fired. This is an unusually high rate, though workers in other countries also raised similar demands.[38] Such strikes were most pronounced in some of the industries in which syndicalist unions were particularly strong, notably metalworking and woodworking, though they were important also in mining, textiles, and printing but not so significant in construction work or food processing.[39] In other words, there is only an incomplete correlation between syndicalism in unions and the high incidence of demands concerning personal issues. Why associate these demands with syndicalism at all? Unusually frequent strikes against hated managers or on behalf of fellow workers might indicate unusual levels of class consciousness and solidarity; this would be consistent with syndicalism whether syndicalism caused the sentiment or merely reflected it. Some of the strikes for or against persons were also intended to express grievances against new methods of work and new units of business organization. We noted earlier that acceptance of syndicalism might express a similar hostility toward the rise of big business, particularly among artisans. Finally, many of the personal clashes resulted from a strong desire among workers for personal dignity and freedom. Syndicalist goals stand out in the labor movement in their urgent and immediate emphasis on freedom. The importance of strikes over personal issues in France is clearly revealed in their increasing incidence during the period, despite the fact that they were more likely to end in defeat than any other major type of strike. Moreover, many strikes that ultimately developed wages or hours demands began in fact in a personal dispute.

Many of the strikes for or against individuals resulted from deeply felt grievances that workers found difficult to phrase in an abstract way. Many workers resented employer efforts to increase the pace of work. The most common protest came when a worker failed or refused to meet the employer demand and was fired. Then his comrades walked out, sometimes simply insisting that he be rehired, sometimes asking that the pace of work be reduced. Metalworkers, whose employers pressed for increased production in the prewar years, often struck against a foreman who had told a worker to speed things up, noting specifically that the order was unfair. Or workers would strike against those of their fellows who accepted a new, more intensive system of work and demand that they be fired. Strikes against foremen by carpenters and cabinetmakers, which were far more frequent than in most crafts, may have resulted from the tension created by the growing size of the units of employment, which violated many worker traditions. The degree of grievance in these strikes is hard to measure since the immediate cause and direct demand were phrased in terms of persons rather than generalities. This was, at best, a primitive way to protest grievances such as the rising pace of work; it may suggest even that workers were not conscious of the problems beyond a vague sense of trouble and were motivated largely by their loyalty to friends.[40]

Fear of unemployment provoked some strikes against women workers or apprentices, with demands for at least a limitation of their numbers. This fear and personal antagonisms prompted a number of strikes against foreign workers. Ditchdiggers and other laborers frequently protested the use of Spanish or Italian workers, claiming that they were too easily exploited or too violent. There was a great deal of agitation against foreigners in eastern France in 1913, because of their widespread use in barracks construction and, probably, an intensified nationalist feeling.[41] These personal strikes were not only primitive but also contrary to any general class solidarity.

Many of the personal-issue strikes manifested at least rudimentary beliefs in labor solidarity. Indeed, strikes against other workers often protested their refusal to accept the values of the main body of labor. It was in personal strikes that workers most often expressed their desire for greater dignity and at least hinted at a need for a direct voice in industrial decisions.

Many workers were willing to strike for fair and polite treatment. Tram conductors wanted greater protection from passengers' complaints.[42] Female workers struck several times against lewd and immoral employers, disregarding, in one case, a foreman's explanation that "the Frenchman is amorous."[43] Workers wanted directors who would take some human interest in them. Their strikes against strict foremen did not result from dislike of intensified work alone. Strikers often acted against a new manager who was not as polite as the previous one; leatherworkers in Chaumont blasted one new director "who was only a financier anxious to get rich as fast as possible."[44] One strike resulted when a manager spoke of "anarchy on the site," for the ditchdiggers (in Paris, interestingly enough) felt that he had accused them of being anarchists.[45] Another occurred when a mining foreman told his workers, "I'll make you piss blood."[46] In still another mining strike over an insult, a miner said his only grievance was "against the actions of certain God-damned little engineers who scorn the human dignity of the miner."[47] The concern with dignity developed widely in the period. Carters wanted to be treated as something more than "beasts of burden";[48] some merchant seaman felt that they were "impelled by a sense of dignity" to "revolt against

our tyrants," and they wanted the world to know that "sailors are not
pariahs, they have the same right as any man to aspire to improve their
lot." [49]

From this sense of worth, workers developed a variety of demands on
employers for greater freedom. Miners, quarry workers, and metallurgical workers in factory towns, along with merchant seamen, most
often sought such freedom explicitly; violent attacks on employers in a
few factory towns were an extreme expression of this desire. Workers
wanted religious and political liberty. Miners in the north often insisted
that foremen distribute work impartially, without favoring conservative
and Catholic miners. Le Creusot metallurgical workers in 1899 put freedom of conscience and abolition of the company's secret police at the
top of their list. Limoges porcelain workers agitated when a Catholic
foreman dismissed a worker for giving his child a civic burial.[50] When
two workers were fired for speeches in union meetings, employees in
Brest and Lorient arsenals struck for "the sacred right" of freedom of
opinion, claiming the right "to remain absolute masters of ourselves outside the arsenals." [51] Miners in Montceau-les-Mines in 1901 asked for
religious freedom and elimination of company spies, and their strike
movement produced a startling change in behavior, showing that new
freedoms could have profound effects. Once they had dared to challenge
their employer's authority they learned to defy other conventions as well:
between 1898 and 1912, baptisms and religious marriages and funerals
declined about 50%—and the birth rate by 66⅔%.[52]

The desire for freedom off the job spread widely. Almost every strike
by waiters involved a demand that they be allowed to wear moustaches.
Merchant seamen struck for the right to eat where they pleased when
their ship was in port. Quarry workers in Argenteuil demanded abolition
of obligatory company housing and canteens.[53] The great metallurgical
strike around Longwy in 1905 stressed the elimination of canteens: "The
canteen is a perpetual millstone around our necks, and if we could
obtain regular pay, twice a month, this would be worth a 1-franc raise,
for we could free ourselves from the canteen." [54] Workers here, as often
elsewhere, asked for accounting of the pension fund, which was based
on withholdings from pay, for worker control of mutual aid groups, and,
especially, for the right to choose their own doctors.[55] Bakers in Lyons
struck against company housing, for this concerned their "liberty as
human beings." [56]

The explosion of strikes among merchant seamen, particularly in
Marseilles, resulted primarily from a desire to gain protection against

the brutality and arbitrary treatment of ship's officers, whose authority was backed directly by the state. The 1904 general strike developed from demands for fairer treatment. Sailors asked, among other things, for a suppression of the "red book," in which any dereliction of duty was recorded and which could serve as the basis for a general blacklisting.[57]

The most frequent strikes for greater freedom were more limited in scope, but they were prompted by the same basic impulse. Many of the strikes over shop rules stressed their harshness and inhumanity. Miners attacked arbitrary fines that served to punish workers for their opinions. And the vast number of protests against foremen resulted from their often-abused power to hire and fire as well as to supervise. In an extreme case, construction workers on the Paris subway claimed the right to choose their own foreman, for they felt he should defend workers' interests and be a member of the union.[58]

Workers in all industrial countries conducted strikes for greater freedom and dignity; French workers seem simply to have done so slightly more often and slightly more explicitly. Perhaps this reflected a general individualism in the French character. It also resulted from the extensive changes in the organization of work during this period, which brought industrial supervision and discipline to many traditional trades for the first time. Syndicalism may also have played a role. In specific strikes like the 1905 uprising by metallurgical workers in Lorraine, syndicalist leaders helped press the demands against institutions such as the canteens that kept workers in subjection and made syndicalist recruitment more difficult. Syndicalists' active promotion of class warfare may have encouraged workers to attack their own employers. French workers were clearly interested in something more than material gains, and syndicalism could serve as an appropriate expression of this.

Again, however, there are problems with this sort of analysis. In the first place, strikes for better treatment drew few participants, except those by metallurgical workers and in the merchant marine, where the employers were unusually authoritarian. This was particularly true in the most common of such strikes, where demands were directed for or against a specific person, for these usually involved only the small band of workers that had directly experienced an insult or who knew the foreman in question. Over 92% of all such strikes affected only one company and the average personal strike involved less than twenty-five workers. Often, in fact, these were scarcely strikes at all, but rather resignations in anger, for the workers knew they had no chance of winning and planned to find another job. So the number of workers involved in all the personal strikes was not large; if such strikes coincided with syndicalism, then, they tend to prove that active syndicalism was at best a small minority movement. Beyond this, most of the strikes for or against people, which necessarily involved a very personal sense of anger, could not easily be translated into a general class-conscious action. Syndicalist leaders, in fact, had frequently to oppose the personal-issue strike, because it was so irrelevant to any general issue and risked damaging the labor movement as a whole. Like union leaders of any type, syndicalists often had to show a worker that his personal grievance was insufficient cause for a strike and sometimes simply invalid, as in the case of one who had been dismissed for frequent absenteeism. It is likely that personal strikes in France were as frequent as they were not because syndicalism encouraged them nor because French workers were especially individualistic, but because the weakness of syndicalist union structure, and the fact that unions had few strike funds to withhold (as a disciplinary measure, for example, against ill-advised strikes) meant that the penchant of workers everywhere to seize on a personal grievance was simply not restrained as quickly in France. German and British workers showed much the same tendency to strike out of personal rage, but on the whole their unions were more successful in holding them back. Only in Britain was class consciousness sufficiently advanced to translate a personal affront into a large-scale strike, as in several walkouts by railway engineers just before World War I against the dismissal of a single employee. France in this period did not make the transition.

It is true that sentiments of personal solidarity and fairness could be turned to the defense of the labor movement and the working class. Strikes on behalf of a dismissed labor leader were far more common than for more abstract issues such as general solidarity or the union itself, but they served something of the same purpose. In 1907 most of the workers in a metallurgical plant in Dôle struck when the union leader was fired, though only about a third of the strikers belonged to the union. They made it plain that their primary purpose was to remedy the unfair dismissal, and they said they were willing to stop all union propaganda in the future. Paris coachmen in one company, only mildly concerned about negotiations to raise their pay, went on a violent strike when their employer insulted and hit their union leader. And many strikes were prolonged until workers were assured that no leader would be dismissed.[59]

This sort of defense of union comrades usually depended on personal attachments, however, and was therefore quite local. And it was difficult to translate personal loyalties into impersonal demands. Characteristically, there were few formal efforts to obtain recognition of a union. According to government statistics, only 1% of all strikes seriously sought union recognition. This figure is undoubtedly too low, but it is true that where the demand was made it was often just an addition to the original list, made at the union's insistence and during the excitement of a strike; equally often it was the first demand to be dropped, if only because workers realized the intensity of employer resistance and feared to compromise their other goals. Some important strikes, such as the metallurgical conflicts at Le Creusot in 1899 and Lorraine in 1905, did focus on union recognition, but this was rare.[60]

Workers often tried also to express their resentment against other workers who had joined neither the strike nor the union, but they rarely sought a union shop. In periods of excitement, as on the Marseilles docks from 1901 to 1904 and in the Paris building trades around 1908, fights with nonunion workers and strikes to exclude them were frequent. In Paris, such strikes were encouraged by the syndicalist unions. These showed signs of a vigorous solidarity; but again, it was hard to develop this solidarity into a more general or impersonal approach. The strikes were usually against specific people whose presence was insupportable, not against nonunion workers generally as a matter of principle. Only a few dockers and truckers (both faced with irregular employment) really tried to get union shops. In the most notable case, on the docks of Sète, workers successfully boycotted any employer who did not accept a union shop and were able to reserve almost all work for the 300 union members, while carefully avoiding any expansion of the union itself.[61]

On the whole, then, the workers' desire for freedom and solidarity, while undeniably vigorous, had little to do with a general class consciousness or with syndicalism. This was small-group loyalty, attachment to comrades or hatred of superiors known and visible to the workers. Most of the strikes on personal issues were unsophisticated, even primitive, their spontaneous outbreak and small size indicating an immature movement. The feelings they expressed may well have served as a basis for later, passionate class feeling in France, but this had not then clearly developed (at least outside the political arena) and did not take syndicalist forms. Finally, when strikes set demands for freedom or solidarity that were more than personal, they revealed that workers could be satisfied with very moderate gains. In this as in other types of demands,

French labor was not ready to hold out for positive improvements of great magnitude.

Hence most strikes that sought any structural changes in employer-worker relations involved demands for formal, written strike settlements and, sometimes, for worker agents or delegations to supervise certain conditions on the job. Often these demands did not involve the unions at all. Mining and textile strikes sometimes insisted on the presence of worker delegates in all weighing or measuring of work, for determination of piece-rate payments; other workers simply asked for representatives who could transmit any complaints directly to the employers.[62] Le Creusot workers, after their bitter strikes, accepted modest labor-management committees (with no union participation) with every appearance of contentment, though we cannot be certain that discontent did not continue to exist secretly. More and more workers of all sorts and their leaders learned that written contracts were vital to protect any strike gains. Construction workers on strike, in Paris and the provinces alike, insisted on contracts after 1906. Quarry workers at Draveil in 1907 said they would moderate their wage demands but would not compromise on the need for a contract. The resulting spread of contracts and workers' representatives on the job were important developments in French industrial relations, but there is little evidence that they signified a positive desire to alter this structure in a radical way. And, of course, insofar as they dealt with employers within the existing system, workers were ignoring the most basic syndicalist impulse. No one can claim that the workers who accepted written contracts did not harbor revolutionary desires which they could not then express; but there is little evidence that they did. There was no rebellion against the collective contract system, as there was to some extent in Britain after 1910; French workers, like the British around 1900, had not then experienced the frustrations of the system. This is one reason that strike rates levelled off in France after 1910, despite prosperity, as they had in Britain in 1899. Even compared to German workers, who long resisted agreements lasting more than a year, French workers accepted a collective bargaining system readily, for despite syndicalist misgivings about the loss of freedom of action, French workers typically sought three-year contracts.[63] And though syndicalist leaders proclaimed their freedom to strike despite contracts to defend labor's general interests and solidarity, they rarely tried to act on this freedom; only in Paris between 1906 and 1909 were contract violations by syndicalist unions frequent, but no more frequent than in Berlin in the same years or in Marseilles earlier.

The Tactics of Moderation: Negotiation

As we have seen, strike demands in France before World War I reveal a conservative, pragmatic labor force. Workers rarely ignored the limits of the possible in their demands and when they did they quickly retrenched. In January 1908, typographers in Mont-de-Marson struck against unemployment. They asked that all women be replaced and that the companies hire local unemployed typographers in preference to all others. They also demanded overtime pay and a cessation of fines, plus the establishment of a committee of employers and workers to resolve future differences. Yet they quickly saw that a raise was all they could win and they settled for this. Few workers ventured such sweeping demands at all. Although the overriding general cause of strikes was the declining real wage, this decline was not severe enough to impart a radical tone to the strike movement.[64]

The nature of strike demands also suggests that many of the possible causes of syndicalism had little reality for most workers. There was little sign of intense anger against the government. Strikes did not reflect a generalized concern about the structure of the economy. The growing size of business units and the spread of machines did not rouse persistent hostility. The most concerned workers, like printers, carpenters, and masons, reduced any uneasiness they felt by seeking higher earnings. Even unemployment was only occasionally noted as a problem; French strikes were directed toward reducing unemployment far less than were British.

Workers clearly had difficulty articulating some of their grievances. In Graulhet in 1907 there was great uneasiness because over half the leather-workers were unemployed, but though several strikes resulted they all raised only immediate and personal demands. Few strikes formally protested machines, but how many workers felt like the Parisian shoemaker who said that "the machine has killed the trade" or like his colleague who proclaimed: "If I want the revolution, it's not to do any harm to people, but to be able to destroy all these machines"?[65] How much syndicalist anger was not specifically expressed because workers were too unsophisticated or too intimidated to bring it forth in strike demands?

The tactics used in strikes on the whole confirm the moderation which strike demands suggest. They were not the product of a high level of inarticulate frustration. Syndicalist doctrine and the violent rhetoric of some syndicalist leaders during strikes had no more influence on the protest methods workers used than on the goals they expressed. Above all, workers' eagerness to negotiate defied any prompting toward all-out class war.

Syndicalists had many misgivings about bargaining in strikes and conducted heated debates on the question. Some argued that the existing system would yield nothing that was not simply seized by force. Others feared that bargaining would tie workers down and inhibit a revolutionary effort (and they were right). In some strikes, a minority of workers, whether out of syndicalist conviction or a visceral hostility to the existing order (which a minority of workers felt in most industrial countries) opposed bargaining. Still more workers were not sure how to bargain or even how to present their demands. But the overwhelming majority of French strikers wanted to negotiate. Employers often rebuffed them and many strikes ended without formal discussions, yet the workers kept trying.

In only a handful of instances did workers refuse to negotiate. After the angry 1906 strike by northern miners, an initial referendum rejected a negotiated settlement, and it took concerted efforts by the unions to win acceptance on a second vote; but this was not of course a rejection of the principle of negotiation. Paris construction workers, in their period of exaltation between 1906 and 1909, who deliberately defied agreements with their employers by striking against nonunion workers or for solidarity with workers elsewhere in violation of contract, never renounced the principle of negotiation. In a few other tense strikes workers rejected outside intervention. Metalworkers in Le Chambon-Feugerolles refused a judge's mediation, stating that "no one other than ourselves is competent to discuss our interests with such arbitrary people [the employers]." [66] Here, as in a similar action by Marseilles dockers in 1904, the memory of an earlier arbitration, which had led to an unsatisfactory settlement, caused the antagonism. But Grenoble glove workers rebuffed a judge and the prefect simply because they were not in the industry, just as the syndicalist press frequently complained that outside intervention inevitably favored the employers because the mediators were all bourgeois. [67] A minority of workers in many other strikes shared similar sentiments, particularly in Paris. In the late stages of a Parisian jewelers' strike, when defections prompted some leaders to urge negotiations, others resisted, claiming that it was against the dignity of the workers to make the first move. In the bitter strike by Parisian taxi drivers in 1912, the strike committee initially sent a list of demands to the companies, swearing that they would never send delegations; it was up to the companies to answer, yes or no. But two months later they had to try to bargain, lest timid workers abandon the strike. In many of the larger and more agitated strikes, a minority usually criticized the pusillanimity of leaders who formally closed a hopeless strike. Some workers, indeed, refused to return to work at all. Approximately 2,300 workers left Le Creusot after the 1900 strike, which had won some gains but had led to the establishment of a powerful company union; thirty workers, the remnant of 312 strikers, refused to return to a Pamiers metallurgical plant.[68]

Some of the recalcitrant workers were syndicalist or open to syndicalism. Many more were not doctrinally motivated but simply furious at a tough employer. Many lost their bitterness after the heat of the strike had passed. Some of the holdouts, particularly in Paris, were unemployed anyway, with nothing to lose if a strike dragged on. The correlation between resistance to negotiation and syndicalism is incomplete. Most important, the recalcitrant workers were only a small minority of active strikers even in syndicalist-led unions. The cases of outright resistance stand out as exceptions.

Most strikes of any size generated active efforts to negotiate. Between 1899 and 1914, over 16% of all strikes involved either formal negotiation, conciliation, or arbitration; and efforts to negotiate informally, that is, without direct union participation, occurred in the majority of strikes.[69]

Many workers went farther still. Dislike of outside intervention was seldom great enough to prevent appeals to state authorities. On this point, too, the vast majority of workers were pragmatic. Workers refused only 2% of the offers of conciliation by justices of the peace, who, under an 1892 law, were given considerable responsibility for mediating labor disputes; and slightly over half of such conciliation procedures were initiated at the request of workers.[70] Though most small strikes were settled without such help, almost all the large or lengthy strikes resulted in some attempt to win government support for negotiation. Strike leaders in Paris, syndicalists especially, appealed directly to a state minister, at least when it became apparent that employers would not bargain or that a major effort was beginning to fail; this occurred even in the eight-hour-day strike in 1906, after the first ten days passed without result. Around 1900 strike committees in the provinces wrote often to Millerand or Waldeck-Rousseau, "in the hope," as metalworkers near Denain said, "that you, M. le Ministre, will be willing to take our demands into consideration and use your high authority . . . to see . . . if you can persuade our employer to grant the eminently fair demands of the workers." [71] Later in the period, faith in the government may have slackened. But if there were fewer appeals to ministers in Paris, there were far more to departmental prefects. Local governments, some of them run by socialists, frequently served as mediators also, as did individual officials such as city architects. Thus, in French strikes there appeared little general sentiment that the state was either irrelevant or completely hostile. Until 1906, over one quarter of all strikes included appeals for state mediation in some form. Strikers knew, at the least, that the government recognized the right to strike almost invariably and that it seldom tried to impose completely unfavorable settlements on the workers.

There was diversity of course. From the very beginning of a Lorette (Loire) metallurgy strike in 1911, strike meetings were filled with bitter condemnation of government repression. The police were assailed for their interference, their patronizing attitude, and their violence, and in one meeting a policeman was badly beaten. At the end of a 1908 strike by miners at Cagnac, the workers voted formal thanks to the government and the prefect for their assistance in guiding and settling the strike.[72] These extremes did not usually obtain.

Violence

Willingness to negotiate is not conclusive proof of moderation. Workers might seek to bargain because they felt weak and intimidated and still harbor deep resentment. Yet such workers, when they could protest at all, would be violent. French strikers were not. The rare cases of significant violence stemmed from intense frustration on the part of workers whose situation was decidedly unusual in France. Furthermore, these workers were remote from syndicalist influence. In this case, clearly, the radical minority was distinct from syndicalism.

Four or five strikes between 1899 and 1914 burst forth with violence against the employer and his property. The situation that prompted this sort of violence, which was really a revolution against a single employer who was a dictator in his factory town, was always basically the same. The setting was isolated; there was little police protection; and this was the first strike the workers had conducted, at least for several years. The employer ran the stores, the local church, and the elections. There was no outside leadership or doctrinal motivation for such strikes. In 1894 and again in 1900, Fressenville lockworkers had tried to set up unions, but all the members were dismissed. They tried again in 1906, with the same result; but this time they struck, and two hours later burned their employer's house down. Neuvilly was a small town near Valenciennes whose principal industry was weaving. The workers were poorly paid, partly in kind, and were sometimes beaten. A union collapsed in 1900, and this led to a reduction in pay; a further reduction in 1904 brought a strike. Workers set up barricades and stoned and burned the employer's house. In 1909 a worker tried to set up a union in a lock factory in Doincourt, but the employer stopped him; a scuffle ensued, in which the employer's son was hurt by a stone. A hundred workers went on strike, stoned the employer's house, burned his furniture, and threatened him with death. There are just a handful of rebellions of this type. Only the rising of 1899 in Montceau-les-Mines was really significant, but though the grievances against the employer were intense the violence occurred here only after the strike had dragged on. The rebellions were spontaneous; syndicalists could capitalize on them in their propaganda, but they had nothing directly to do with them.[73]

Aside from these cases, the most important labor violence occurred after the frustrations of months of fruitless striking, when the grievances that provoked the strike, themselves intensely felt, were exacerbated by increasing misery and, usually, by the presence of police and army patrols. In these cases, speeches by particularly excited workers, some of them syndicalists, often played a role, but syndicalist leaders were seldom involved. In Saint-Léger-des-Domart, 160 dismissed textile workers, goaded by hunger after a long strike, attacked their factory and destroyed many machines, shouting, "We must have bread or blood." [74] Employers' efforts to return some workers to their jobs, import new workers, and set up company unions often added to the tension. It was after 450 workers joined an independent union in Le Chambon-Feugerolles during a particularly bitter metallurgical strike that bombs were set at two employers' homes. Graulhet leatherworkers in 1910 attacked carts bringing supplies to the factories, and women lay on the road to prevent their passage; later, explosions were set off in several employers' homes.[75] Usually violence in the late stages of a strike primarily expressed frustration at an employer's refusal to negotiate. A mob often developed from a crowd assembled to hear an employer's response that never came or that was unfavorable. In Lille in 1903, 6,000 textile workers rioted when they learned that manufacturers had not answered their demands. They roamed all over town looking for their employers, seized and burned cloth in the factories, and in the evening blocked off streets and doused street lights to impede the police, and then set many fires. In 1907, 230 dockers in Tornay, furious at their inability to win any negotiation, seized their employer at the city hall and tied him up in the union office until he signed a contract.[76]

These actions were important. They were no more frequent in France than elsewhere. For the most part they reflected the excitement of the moment rather than deep class hatred on the part of the workers. Often such strikes ended within a few days after the violence took place, for most of the strikers grew ashamed of their own excesses and fearful of the impact on public opinion. Finally, few of the cases of violence involved workers in syndicalist unions. There is, overall, no positive correlation between syndicalist leadership and significant violence in strikes. This points up not only the reluctance of most syndicalist leaders to urge violence in actual strikes but also the fact that the members of most syndicalist unions were unusually sophisticated and restrained in tactics. The most generalized violence in the whole period occurred in Armentières in 1903, when thousands of poor linen weavers pillaged stores and banks; insofar as these people were in unions at all, the unions were socialist-led. And whatever the type of union involved, violence was usually spontaneous, influenced indirectly at most by doctrines or excited speeches. Violence could not be planned on a large scale. Syndicalist leaders tried hard in 1911 to spread protests against food prices, after the spontaneous attacks on merchants in several northern cities. They uniformly failed, whether they hinted at violence or not; lukewarm meetings of a few hundred workers were the best they could do in any city.[77]

Barbers, waiters, and bakers, particularly in Paris, conducted the strikes in which syndicalism was most clearly linked to violence. Urged by the union leaders, workers between 1904 and 1906 tossed acid on shop fronts during agitation against employers who refused to grant a weekly day off. Even here, it was often young, unemployed day laborers, not the unionized workers, who struck. Paris, like Liverpool and Berlin, had a number of toughs ready to turn a strike into a pretext for violence; most of the largest clashes with police were similarly conducted by a cross section of local toughs, not primarily by strikers themselves. It is, again, not clear that syndicalism influenced these people; their youth, their experience with jobs that required physical strength, and their frequent unemployment were more significant causes. And the strikes by barbers and bakers were exceptional cases, brought about by the weakness of the unions and the inability to win strikes by ordinary means.[78]

The 1910 railroad strike might seem to introduce important qualifications to this picture of syndicalist tameness. Prior to this strike, the talk of sabotage, common enough in syndicalist unions, was translated into more precise recommendations. Second-level syndicalist leaders, like

Louis Le Guennic, urged the railroad workers to commit acts of sabotage, and a pamphlet full of specific suggestions was widely distributed. These agitators, again particularly around Paris, were fighting a conservative, nonsyndicalist union leadership. They knew that the railroad companies were tough and that most workers, particularly in the provinces, were reluctant to strike. So they sought supplementary weapons. From the beginning of the strike, and particularly after the government mobilized the railroad workers, significant acts of sabotage occurred, though again they were committed by general laborers as well as by strikers. Between October 8 and 21, 1,411 acts of sabotage were reported, 1,035 of them on the Nord line, where excitement had been highest. In the next three months there were 912 sabotage efforts, and for some time thereafter strikes by ditchdiggers and other laborers included some wire cutting. This sabotage undeniably shows syndicalist influence as well as worker frustration. But most of the acts were relatively minor; of the 1,411 cases that occurred during and soon after the strike, 1,187 involved cutting telegraph and telephone wires (the remainder included 10 shots fired, 11 attempted bombings, 30 stonings of trains, 64 blocked signals, and 82 attempted derailments). Significantly, most of the acts were carried out by individuals or small groups. The vast majority of railroad strikers did not participate; the whole effort, despite much propaganda, was in a way rather meager. And it was decidedly atypical of French labor protest as a whole. Sabotage efforts, for most workers, were too radical; even for angry workers, their effects were too diffuse to express precise grievances. They certainly did not further a strike.[79]

Prior to the British railroad strike a year later, in 1911, there were no general recommendations of sabotage, and syndicalism had little if any influence. Yet this strike was far more violent than its French predecessor. More trains were stoned, more signal boxes destroyed. Often, bands of 200 or more workers were involved. On the Great Western Line alone, 7 engines were damaged along with 44 other vehicles, 96 wagons were looted, 6 signal boxes destroyed, and several warehouses burned or looted. To be sure, only 17 wires were cut, but this was because the workers had bigger projects in mind. And there was nothing in France in this period to compare to the virtual revolution of dockers, railroad workers, and miners in Wales from 1910 to 1911; workers here attacked, not only company property, but also Jewish storekeepers, Chinese laundrymen, and local magistrates.[80] The closest French counterpart to this, the riot by Armentières weavers in 1903, is not in the same class. British workers were truly angry; French workers were not. Hence revolutionary syndicalism could not impel French workers toward violence.

Violence against workers who refused to join a strike, who returned to work prematurely, or who served as outright strikebreakers was far more common than attacks on property or employers. Even in this respect, most individual strikes were fairly calm. And the type of violence involved, including the goals implied, was less significant than the disruption which burst through the framework of the strikes. But attacks on other workers often indicated intense grievance. Some of them led to clashes with police who tried to protect the beseiged workers. Syndicalist leaders were often involved. Was there a correlation between this sort of violence and syndicalism?

Syndicalist leaders, as we have seen, particularly in the Parisian construction workers' strikes before 1910, certainly urged the "fox hunt." All the major construction strikes in Paris until shortly before the war brought attacks on individual workers by bands of strikers and invasions of work sites by groups of ten to 150 workers, who stoned or beat their reluctant fellows, broke tools, and dismantled some of the work in progress. In the May 1, 1906, strike in Paris, ninety-eight policemen were injured when they tried to impede these attacks and more general demonstrations. Syndicalists definitely played a role here, at least by their general denunciations of police repression in strike meetings. Syndicalist leaders were likewise involved in a riot by 1,000 silk workers in Voiron against strikebreakers brought in from Lyons; this turned into a major clash with the 600 policemen who were there to protect the strikebreakers.

Against the notion of a special syndicalist role, however, several points must be raised. First, this sort of violence was typical of all the industrial countries. Workers everywhere were bitter against colleagues who refused to strike and against policemen who impeded them. If anything, the French were as usual relatively moderate. There were no more strikers and policemen killed in France than in England after 1899, despite the fact that French police presence was far more common and police methods more provocative. Nothing in France could compare to the battle between strikers and police and nonstrikers in the Ruhr mines in 1912. From a comparative standpoint, the notion of a special syndicalist influence on violence against workers and police rests, once again, on an examination of the construction workers' strikes in Paris between 1906 and 1909, which can hardly lead to very general claims. Moreover the Parisian violence fits the general pattern of major construction strikes, such as those in Berlin in 1906–1907 and elsewhere in Germany in 1910. For violence against other workers stemmed largely from the strike situation itself, regardless of whether leaders urged it, as in Paris, or deplored it, as in Berlin. Finally, even within France, this sort of violence was most common among workers who were not syndicalist.

Miners' strikes, particularly in the nonsyndicalist north, usually involved attacks on workers until after 1906. Dockers in the major strikes were still more violent. Some were armed and willing to face the police (which bands of construction workers usually avoided) as well as other workers. The chief causes of this kind of violence were the nature and location of work. Everywhere, work in scattered sites, like building lots or mines, forced workers who wanted to spread their strike to roam in potentially violent bands. If Parisian construction workers were more violent than their provincial comrades, it was due less to syndicalism than to the unusual dispersion of construction sites in a big city. Violence came also from workers whose labor was physically demanding to an unusual degree and who (miners excepted here) faced unusually long and frustrating periods of unemployment. Hence young dockers, ditchdiggers, and day laborers provided much of the violence in other urban strikes as well as their own. A strike by Saint-Étienne ribbon weavers in 1900 led to an attack on renegade workers and then to a fight with police; but by the time the riot had gone this far the weavers had returned home, and their place was taken by a general city mob, with construction laborers the most prominent element. Of the 67 people arrested in the 1903 Armentières riot, only 14 were weavers, while 20 were laborers or unemployed. In Paris violent crowds were occasionally more broadly based, which might suggest syndicalist influence but is more likely a symptom of general radical sentiment; men arrested for attacking police in a strike by Paris tailors in 1901 included a salesman, two mechanics, two students, a musician, four clerks, a lawyer, a bellboy, a journalist, a house painter, a fur worker, an unemployed laborer, and one tailor.[81] Only a few types of workers were normally apt to be violent, whether they seemed syndicalist or not, and these types were no more numerous in France than elsewhere.

Syndicalists could not dent the moderation of French workers in tactics or in demands. Yet even this is not the whole story. Syndicalists had to encourage still further moderation in tactics. They had to combat excited minorities who were their best potential clients. Because the gap between French workers and syndicalism was unbridgeable, the gap between syndicalists' practice and their theory widened steadily.

3 The Failure of Syndicalism

"One cannot regulate a strike, because it is born of a specific fact and almost always spontaneously." [1] Union leaders constantly complained of the carefree attitude of many workers, particularly new union members and nonmembers, who had no sense of the opportuneness of a strike or the need to draw up demands to serve as a basis for agitation. Syndicalist campaigns of course encouraged this immoderate zeal for combat. Many workers who struck for the first time in the 1906 movement for an eight-hour day, for example, were supremely confident that they could gain victory within three days. But campaigns by socialist or even bread-and-butter unions led to great excitement also and spurred many spontaneous strikes. The belief in sudden, unorganized strikes had little to do with syndicalism. German workers were more given to spontaneity than French. Roubaix textile workers, not at all syndicalist, gave their leaders far more trouble with spontaneous strikes than did workers under syndicalist influence. [2]

Syndicalist leaders had to combat spontaneous strikes as other labor organizers did and for the same reasons. The spontaneous strike threatened labor organization. The issues involved seldom roused more than a few dozen workers. In 1907 a construction foreman was dismissed at Grazac. The fifty workers under him, highly indignant, walked out; but their colleagues under other foremen ignored them or, intimidated, went home for a day with every intention of returning on the morrow. The issue involved had no meaning for them and they thought, quite correctly, that the timing (in midwinter) was poorly chosen. [3] Strikes of this sort easily failed because of their poor planning and small size, and any organization involved with them, even involuntarily, could suffer from the defeat. Strikers might split between a minority of excited zealots and a disillusioned majority, hampering the future activities of a trade union. A host of other problems, from dissipation of union funds to the sheer distraction of union leaders by the administration of frequent strikes, arose out of the spontaneous protests of these years. As a consequence many syndicalists railed against the strike movement: "instead of wasting this energy without result, isn't it preferable to organize the general strike directly?" [4] This mood of disillusionment, common before 1902 and the commitment to fomenting strikes, spread again around 1910 as a result of experience. Most leaders, however, recognized that French workers would reject any movement that refused to back their strikes and tried simply to impose some restraint. They were trapped. They had organizations and clientele. They decided to defend them. Defense against the consequences of unwise strikes involved strengthening organizations and resisting the impulse to use distinctively radical tactics.

Furthermore, the workers wanted moderate tactical guidance above all. Their excitement was temporary, often the product of inexperience. They sought, as we have seen, moderate goals and rarely needed much advice on this score. But they were at a loss over tactics, and this is how labor movements gained a role in their protest. Some workers, caught up in a strike without real leadership, tried to carry on by themselves, often because they feared outside radicals. There was a common feeling, particularly around 1900, that only "real workers" should conduct agitation. But most strikers who knew where to turn for assistance appealed for help. They accepted aid from any quarter, because of their desperate need for tactical guidance, not because of ideological commitment. They were especially afraid of trying to deal with their employers on their own. Hence all sorts of outsiders played a role in strikes, including newspaper editors, shopkeepers, and doctors. But workers usually turned to the trade union in their industry or to the C.G.T. as the most visible guide in such matters. Demands for assistance from the C.G.T. and the regional and national union federations increased steadily. Often the launching of a spontaneous strike was followed by a quick march to union headquarters to seek guidance or, in the more remote areas, by a telegram to Paris. And in the important strikes, would-be leaders presented themselves unasked and sometimes took an important role. Anarchists flocked to big strikes early in the period. There were over two hundred, mostly outsiders, at Le Creusot in 1900; workers' families named several dozen children after Maxence Roldes, the best orator among them. Soon, of course, syndicalist leaders similarly moved into all major protest efforts. Because of the syndicalists' lack of bureaucracy there were not enough leaders to go around and they thus lost many opportunities. In 1902 the C.G.T. sent thirteen delegates to nine different strikes, a tiny handful of the disputes that had produced appeals for help. Still, in their hunger for leadership, thousands of workers were temporarily exposed to syndicalism during strikes. Syndicalist leaders who had genuine contact with the workers became skilled strike tacticians.[5]

The temptation to make provocative speeches during strikes persisted.[6] C.G.T. leaders with anarchist backgrounds were less moderate than national federation chiefs. Theoreticians like Georges Yvetot or Émile Pouget found it difficult to urge restraint, whereas federation leaders like Alphonse Merrheim or Victor Griffuelhes typically did so. Only a few federation representatives consistently counseled distinctive tactics. The leaders of the two pitiably weak unions, the barbers' and bakers', saw no virtue in restraint for they could not win an ordinary strike. Occasionally, representatives of the construction workers' federation, dealing with aroused day laborers who had no union experience, yielded to the spirit of the moment. In a final, more familiar case, second-level leaders of the railwaymen in the Paris area advocated sabotage before the 1910 strike. In general, however, syndicalists urged sober tactics in practice, in response to the moderate sentiments of most French workers. Gradually advice from labor leaders and this basic moderation plus growing experience in strike movements combined to alter the character of French strikes.

Syndicalists as Strike Leaders

Actual syndicalist strike tactics can be briefly summarized because they were not unusual at all. The leaders had to maintain the enthusiasm of the initial strikers, extend the strike, and prevent defections—all difficult tactical problems in even partially spontaneous strikes.

The first problem was money. Strikers who appealed to syndicalist leadership wanted not only tactical guidance but funds. Unions constantly received telegrams that starkly stated "strike called, send money" —even from nonmembers. Many strikes, launched with great enthusiasm, were ended when the strikers realized to their horror that they had almost nothing but their own resources to support the effort; and syndicalism suffered not only from the loss of a strike but from the fact that many of the strikers quit their union in anger at the lack of aid. New union members and even nonmembers were notorious for their inflated visions of union funds and their prompt surrender when their illusions were dispelled.[7] A leader of the Fédération du bâtiment noted that it was useless for him to go to a strike without funds to distribute: "No money, no strike."[8] Syndicalist leaders conducting a strike had to spend much of their time seeking money. They learned to build up union funds in advance. Syndicalist unions roughly tripled their dues between 1900 and 1914; after 1908 most major federations had set amounts of strike aid. In the process distinctions between union members and non-members became ever clearer. Syndicalist leaders, like most early union organizers, were initially inclined to try to aid all strikers. By 1908 they were stipulating that only members of six months' standing received full assistance. It is true that funds and strike aid were still relatively low by 1914. The syndicalist tradition left its mark. Syndicalist unions were well on the way to better funding, however, and fewer strikers were left to their own resources. This development was more important and more general than the special syndicalist tactics to support strikes, notably the "communist soups."

The attention to financing influenced many other facets of strike tactics. In particular, syndicalist leaders had to be careful not to offend that amorphous thing called public opinion. In any large strike, the majority of strikers were essentially moderate and sensitive to any public hostility. Many strikes ended when "the public" was alienated by excessive strike demands or acts of violence; public favor was essential to morale. Given their poverty, French unions depended heavily on public favor to obtain funds. Many groups and individuals contributed to strikes, ranging from radical republicans to peasants who brought food. But the shopkeepers were the most important group, providing the most immediate financial aid to strikers, in credit if not in outright grants. It is clear that French strikes operated in a more favorable public climate than was true elsewhere, chiefly because many shopkeepers, with leftist political traditions, sympathized with the workers and were hostile to big business. This is one reason that the syndicalist unions could get by so long with inadequate strike funds of their own. But the shopkeepers and the public in general were opposed to unreasonable demands or tactics, and syndicalist leaders were well aware of this.[9]

The question of funds was intimately linked to the more general problem of spreading a strike and preventing defections. It was difficult to win a strike when only part of the workers in a factory or even in a whole local industry walked out, for employers often kept the work going without them or replaced them altogether. So syndicalist leaders had to promote demands of general import, which usually meant wage demands. They had to make sure that an excited minority did not antagonize a moderate majority by acts of violence as well as by excessive demands, even when the minority was, at least for the moment, drawn to syndicalist doctrines. It is ironic that the syndicalists had to be especially cautious because their poverty deprived them of the easiest means to spread and maintain a strike, the ample daily payment.[10]

From the first, syndicalist leaders realized that the moderate majority had to be represented on strike committees. A minority, whether it was syndicalist or just unusually aroused, could not be allowed to take over. Moderates (including nonunion members and sometimes housewives) were given a say. This, of course, influenced other strike tactics, for the moderates typically worked for realistic bargaining and a quick end to the strike. True, the conduct of strike meetings, with their voice votes, permitted an aroused minority to shout down opposition and prolong a strike; but syndicalists modified this tradition in favor of more extensive, secret consultation.

French strikes were not, in fact, unusually long in this period, compared to patterns in other countries. Over 50% of all strikes ended in less than five days, while only 12% lasted more than a month. German strikes were considerably longer; 19% lasted more than thirty days in the first years of the century.[11] The relatively short duration of strikes in France resulted from three factors. Employers, weakly organized, often had to yield quickly. Most workers, because their intentions were moderate, were willing to compromise and even to abandon a hopeless strike. Labor organizers, syndicalists included, pushed in the same direction. Very few yielded to the temptation to hold out against a nasty employer or against capitalism in general. In most strikes of importance a few workers (including, of course, the unemployed who wanted a continuance of strike aid) sought to prolong the strike unduly. Syndicalist leaders normally realized that undue prolongation would wreck the strike, for most workers would simply go back to work, which would damage the credibility of the union in most workers' eyes. So in this case, too, like most labor leaders, they tried to impose increasing discipline.

Hence, despite their debates over the issue in union congresses, syndicalists tried to negotiate with employers whenever possible. They pursued this policy from the point at which they turned to the active support of strikes in 1902. They tried to teach workers how to negotiate and how to draw up lists of demands and thus reduce the number of strikes that began without a bargaining effort because workers did not know how to go about it or feared that their employer, more articulate and experienced, would gull them into submission. They rarely refused the common plea for assistance in negotiation. They urged workers to bargain even before they struck, in order to avoid needless conflict. They readily accepted compromise in strikes and refused to cater to the minority that resisted this process. They were as willing as were most workers to use state assistance. They had some difficulty arranging this in practice, because government officials not surprisingly considered them troublemakers. But they often appealed for state mediation and toward the end of the period frequently met with officials to discuss their plans for conducting a strike. The result of their use of the state was often anomalous. Time and time again a syndicalist-led strike meeting would excoriate the police and the perversity of the whole government and then break up so that strike leaders could see the prefect or a minister to urge their aid in negotiations and possibly the fulfillment of a new labor law. The most extreme federation leaders, in the barbers' and bakers' unions, were most inclined to appeal for government help, particularly in enforcing the law that provided one day of rest a week.

Syndicalist leaders tried to guard against violence in strikes, for the standard organizational reasons.[12] Not only were most workers antagonized by violence, because they were not radical, but also violence resulted in a police repression that directly threatened the existence of worker organizations. Throughout the period syndicalists used demonstrations, sometimes daily, to keep hotheads out of trouble as well as to show the power of a strike and to boost flagging spirits. This was the motive of the still-revolutionary Aristide Briand when he led 20,000 miners on an exhausting walk from Saint-Étienne to Firminy in the 1902 strike. Leaders like Dret, of the leatherworkers' federation, and Merrheim invariably spoke against violence—sometimes to the bemusement of police spies. Merrheim sought to calm aroused filemakers in Le Chambon in 1911, devoting most of his speeches to the need for prudence, though without complete success.[13] The C.G.T. representative Barthey, speaking to striking leatherworkers in Graulhet, summed up the syndicalists' policy: "You can cut wires, unload wagons, but this won't end the strike. An agreement will result only from discussion." [14]

The tactics syndicalists used in strikes did not necessarily contradict their doctrines. There was always the general strike still to come and this should not be compromised by abortive partial efforts. The goal was to win small strikes in order to teach workers their power and avoid damaging their morale. Negotiation and nonviolence were necessary to vic-

tory, so they were used. But in the process the strike movement became
still more moderate. Workers withdrew still further from real syndicalist
influence. Even some of the most excitable types of workers were calming
down.

Causes of Change in Strike Activity

A harsher atmosphere for strikes was the most obvious cause of changes
in the protests. Government and employer policy stiffened after 1906.
Hence violence became more dangerous to the workers, failure to negotiate realistically more self-defeating. This new environment merely supported the moderation of most workers; it did not bring a basic change
in mood but it did change their tactics. Only the syndicalist leaders and
the minority of workers who followed them, particularly in Paris, were
visibly perturbed. For, after all, a harsher environment could have produced an angrier strike movement, as was the case in these same years
in England and to an extent even in Germany. Instead, French workers
accepted the limitations of the new situation. And the new situation was
not entirely unfavorable to them in terms of their expectations. Along
with greater repression by employers came increased collective bargaining. Also, previous strike movements had brought real gains to many
groups: tobacco and match workers won pay raises of 20% to 30% by
strike and union action; Paris ditchdiggers achieved a 40% raise between
1905 and 1908; printers obtained city-wide wage rates and reductions in
working hours in 150 cities; and so on. New laws, induced by strikes,
banned private employment bureaus, company canteens, and excessive
withholdings from pay; miners and maritime workers had won special
legal protection for their hours of work.[15] Added to such gains after 1910
was the end of the decline in real wages and a reduction in levels of
unemployment. The second reason for the changing character of strikes
was, then, the contentment of increasing numbers of workers. Finally,
again given the moderation of the French labor force, growing experience
with unions and with labor agitation taught the workers to restrain their
enthusiasms; in this the promptings of syndicalists as well as other labor
leaders played an important role. Union members were involved in
barely half of all strikes in 1899; by 1913 they figured in almost 80% of
them. More strikes, therefore, were subject to a union's tactical guidance,
while the unions, increasingly involved in strikes, had even more reason than before to counsel prudence.

The most important indication of the new trends in strike activity was the growing rate of strike failures. By 1913, strike failures occurred a full third more frequently than they had in 1906, and both victories and compromise settlements had declined at an approximately equal rate. The decline in successful strikes began, admittedly, with an economic recession in 1908–1909, but it continued even when prosperity returned; economic factors were not primarily responsible.[16] All types of strike demands suffered from the new trends; even movements for pay raises, long one of the easiest goals to win, failed outright about 4% oftener, while efforts to reduce the number of working hours suffered even more dramatically. Between 1899 and 1907 a strike had about a 65% chance of winning at least a compromise settlement; after this, it had little more than a 50–50 prospect.[17]

This development most obviously reflected the new tough stand of employers and government. Many workers undoubtedly grew more afraid to strike. Within the affected work-group, rates of participation in strikes declined dramatically, which further reduced the chances of success. But fear was not the only element involved here. One of the reasons that strike victories declined was that some of the most alert workers, those best able to conduct a protest, were gaining satisfaction without a strike, through collective bargaining or the more favorable movement of the economy as a whole. It was notable that though strikes became more sophisticated in many ways, as we shall see, their average size decreased after 1907 (though it later rose again slightly). The recrudescence of small strikes meant that agitation was spreading to new groups of workers, who were inexperienced and relatively weak, while some of the better organized workers no longer had to strike so often. Even the percentage of union members involved in strikes, though it rose markedly in the period as a whole, declined somewhat after 1905. Because of growing satisfaction on the part of workers who had always been moderate, strikes were taken over by the less organized and less experienced elements. But even these workers were pragmatic and often open to increasingly cautious union guidance. One other statistical change in the characteristics of the strike movement was significant: the average strike became shorter. Despite the growing rigidity of the employers, workers were less willing than before to hold out for their demands. They were not interested in intensifying their protest. They remained moderate, while experience and union leadership taught them that a long strike was rarely worth the effort. All these factors—the harsher environment, the growing contentment of many workers, and the effects of greater experience in labor agitation—must be assessed.

After 1906 workers could not look to the central government for the sort of sympathy that they had often expected from ministers like Waldeck-Rousseau or Millerand. Only a few strikers appealed to Clemenceau, "France's leading cop," for assistance in negotiations; after Briand brutally rejected the railroad workers' request for arbitration in 1910, he too was free from such demands. Bloody police repression of striking quarry workers in Draveil and Villeneuve-Saint-Georges in 1908 and 1910 and the firm action taken against the railroad strike undoubtedly discouraged workers still further. This sort of pressure contributed to the increasing caution of unions in supporting activities that might lead to violence, and, perhaps, in calling strikes at all. Repression increased particularly in Paris, though police surveillance had always been heavy there; the actions of 1908–1910 had focused on the Paris area, where the C.G.T. was strongest and where protests in Parliament about labor's highhandedness were most intense. Several of the leaders of major federations and of the C.G.T. were arrested in this period. Construction unions began to note that police protection of "renegade" workers had increased, notably through a more complete supervision of individual building sites. Finally, public opinion in many areas turned against the strikers; shopkeepers, particularly, grew less sympathetic. This raised problems of morale and forced more attention to the unions' financial support of strikes.[18]

However, government pronouncements about strikes probably changed more than actual policy did in ordinary circumstances and in the provinces. The familiar shows of force should not be confused with the policies that touched most workers directly, for the evolution of the latter was slight and in many ways favorable to labor. There were no signs in strikes that workers had turned against the government. Official government directives about handling strikes remained the same. In 1913 prefects were urged to mediate every possible strike, to avoid violence and to resolve all issues fairly. There is no general indication that troops were used more frequently or more massively—the numbers introduced in dockers' and miners' strikes actually declined and they were used less conspicuously. Prefects played an increasingly active role in facilitating negotiations, and though they discouraged unions from some unwise strikes they also moderated employer action. The prefect of Ille-et-Vilaine kept active contacts with labor and management in Fougères during and after the 1914 strike in a way that had not been attempted in the 1906–1907 outburst. This helped eliminate violence and also resulted in a more successful strike than before. Similar prefectoral action helped moderate miners' strikes in the Loire; again the effect was a change of method rather than less success. Workers felt at least as free as before to appeal to prefects and subprefects for assistance in bargaining. At most, the official encouragement of bargaining may have reduced the need for the better-organized workers to strike and so left the strike field open to small efforts by workers who were likely to lose.[19]

One change in state action decisively reduced chances of success in strikes, particularly in the case of minor strikes, but apparently not as the result of official government policy. The number of conciliation attempts under the 1892 law, mainly under the auspices of justices of the peace, declined drastically from 1904 on. This conciliation occurred in almost 25% of all strikes until 1904 and usually brought at least a compromise settlement; between 1907 and 1913, such conciliation dropped to a range of 2% to 8% of all strikes.[20] The government did not discourage these procedures, though it promoted the intervention of prefects to take up the slack. The chief reasons for the change were the growing reliance of workers on their unions instead of on outsiders for negotiation and the growing reluctance of magistrates, who shared the public hostility toward strikes and unions, to interfere with employers' tactics. The result was that small and poorly organized strikes had much less chance of winning than before. In sum, by 1913 strikers had to count on a new public climate, which various levels of government shared to some degree; but so long as their tactics were moderate, they probably faced less government repression than before.

The policies of manufacturers changed far more than those of the government. Most manufacturers had been caught off guard by the rising wave of strikes and strike victories in the first years of the century, but by 1905 they had begun to learn that new defensive measures were needed. They resented the cost of concessions to strikers, for even in a prosperous year these could reduce profits, as wage raises granted to dockers did for the Compagnie générale transatlantique in 1900. Furthermore, manufacturers feared that instability would increase without firmer resistance; many of them experienced not only mounting strike rates but also growing indiscipline on the job before they finally took action.[21] The lockout on the Marseilles docks in 1904 was motivated above all by the desire for "serious and definitive guarantees of stability in work." [22]

The reaction to strikes was often individual, an intensification of earlier efforts to dismiss agitators and outlast strikes. The most effective response to the new strike threat, however, was collective. Hesitantly, manufacturers began to unite for defense. Hat manufacturers decided in 1911 to oppose worker discipline with discipline of their own, and they set up a conciliation committee to prevent strikes and a blacklist to punish workers who struck anyway. Calais tulle producers joined in 1900 to subdue a strike; 324 out of a total of 352 united to set up a strike fund and, if necessary, to join in a lockout. The movement spread to all types of manufacturers. Construction contractors in Cyamax (Allier) formed a union after several small strikes. The larger Parisian masonry contractors did the same in 1908, after a rash of disturbances. The number of employer associations almost tripled between 1897 and 1913, reaching a total of 5,063, while membership rose in the same proportions to 421,566. Not all the groups were designed to combat strikes and many of them were weak. Large manufacturers were much more closely united than were small manufacturers, which helps explain the continued persistence of tiny strikes against tiny firms. But the movement was general and it significantly reduced the chances for strikers to win.[23]

When provoked by repeated agitation, employers organized lockouts, often combined with the formation of a paternal union. Fougères shoe manufacturers locked out 8,000 workers in 1906–1907; Parisian construction companies staged lockouts in 1908 for ditchdiggers and in 1909 for about half of the city's masons; Marseilles maritime firms locked out 6,000 dockers in 1904. The Marseilles firms also set up a collective union to employ a minority of workers with assurances of regular employment and other benefits. Later, Marseilles trucking firms and dock companies in other cities imitated the effort, which had considerable success in dividing workers, whose greatest concern was stable employment. Parisian masonry contractors tried the same ploy in 1909, but with less decisive results.[24]

This new toughness, which so visibly succeeded in defeating increasing numbers of strikes, might have furthered class consciousness and class hatred. Undoubtedly some workers were confirmed in their syndicalism by their employers' obduracy, even if they were impotent to strike, and many turned to political attacks on the harsh system which strikes alone could not overturn. Many more, however, along with their union leaders, tried to develop appropriate new forms of strike action. Though their discussion outdistanced their practical action new tactics resulted. Parisian masons tightened up their union organization after 1909; Marseilles dockers, whose union began to revive only in 1909, similarly had abandoned excited agitation in favor of well-planned efforts. This evolution toward greater moderation was aided by new opportunities for industrial bargaining.[25]

For repression was not the manufacturers' only response to labor agitation. Conciliatory measures satisfied some workers and removed the need for others to strike; again, the rising rate of strike failure was partly due to the reduced rate of agitation among better-organized workers. Few manufacturers relied on coercion alone. Some granted benefits of their own accord to avoid protest; others provided means for negotiation as an alternative to strikes. The Le Creusot company union, successful in inhibiting agitation after 1900, constituted a genuine channel for the presentation of worker grievances; an average of 300 demands a year over working conditions and wages were negotiated, with two thirds of them fully satisfied. The collective paternal unions, like the one organized by Marseilles truckers, had mixed committees of employers and workers to settle disputes.[26] Le Chambon manufacturers, bitterly opposed to the metalworkers' union, agreed in 1910 to establish a mixed committee for conciliation on which union members could serve.[27]

Other employers realized that direct negotiation with unions and the establishment of collective contracts had real advantages in the regularization of work. Only after 1902 were more than one or two strikes directly negotiated by manufacturers and unions without outside intermediaries. In 1904, 6% of all strikes were negotiated and in 1905, 12.4%. The percentage did not again reach that level until 1914, as the involvement of union members in strikes dropped and employers found other means of defense; but a significant minority of strikers found direct negotiation still possible. Hence rates of strike failure for union members rose much less rapidly than the general rates. Most important, the number of negotiations continued to increase, and negotiation often prevented strikes altogether.[28] Collective bargaining especially helped to dispose of many personal grievances that had motivated strikes even among unionized workers before. Bargaining did not result in massive improvements in wages or conditions, with some important exceptions; overall real wages rose only slowly after 1910 and the workers' share in national income continued to decline. But, for French workers as a whole, a new level of expectations had to develop before the limitations on collective bargaining were acutely felt. In the meantime the reduction of personal disputes in the best-organized industries, such as mining and construction, curtailed discontent. As workers welcomed collective bargaining and their leaders encouraged it, syndicalism became still less relevant as a distinctive force. Where bargaining was impossible, workers and their leaders became more cautious, because of the growing resistance on the part of manufacturers. Only the basic moderation of the workers remained constant, which allowed the adoption of new tactics as the situation changed and experience grew but did not necessitate a real change of mood in the labor force as a whole.

Nature of the New Tactics

The general theme of the new tactics was restraint, usually through more careful preparation and organization of strikes. As late as 1913 many workers were striking for the first time without knowing how to proceed, but even they caught the spirit of their more experienced brethren. With growing vigor, congresses of the leading federations criticized strikes of anger, in which no effort was made to negotiate beforehand and no basis established for discussions later. Hence, after 1906, fewer strikes began without a clear list of grievances, and the list itself grew smaller. It was notable that after 1906, when over a third of all strikes issued more than one major demand, efforts were more often concentrated on a single goal.[29] Ironically, the eight-hour-day campaign of 1906 proved to be a significant break in the conduct of strikes, in that the unions provided both the issue and the timing for a major effort.

The important strikes by Parisian construction workers and by typographers all over France were more or less under union control from then onward. Even though the lockout of Parisian masons in 1909 was not a complete success for the contractors, for example, the number of small strikes for raises dropped off significantly thereafter. Unions gained the power to limit spontaneous striking in many other industries. Shoe workers in Fougères struck infrequently between the 1906 lockout and the general strike of 1914, whereas before 1906 there had been a rash of small walkouts. General strikes among northern textile workers began on union order after 1909, in contrast with the agitation of 1903 and 1904. Miners' unions gained control over spontaneous strikes after 1906. By 1912 the Marseilles seamen's union was able to prepare a strike and hold it back until the moment of peak employment.[30] While workers learned to wait for a formal strike call, union leaders grew more adept at providing issues for a widespread strike and even anticipating a strike situation,[31] as the northern miners' union did in 1913 when it turned rising tension to its own account by calling a strike against overtime work. As one union leader noted in 1909, the goal was clear: "A maturely conceived strike, prepared in all its details, on a well-chosen date."[32]

The improvement of strike funds increased the unions' power over strikers before and during a strike. From 1909, construction unions in Paris provided regular strike aid to all authorized efforts, which obviously furthered their ability to limit spontaneous strikes. The Fougères shoe workers' union in 1913 began assembling funds and arranging for support from other unions for a strike predicted for five months later. It had 60,000 francs in hand and pledges for 18,500 more per week by the time the strike began. This meant that each striker could be paid four francs a week almost indefinitely and obviously contributed to the calmness of the strike itself.[33]

Careful consultation before a strike began represented another decisive change in tactics that guaranteed greater calm in protest. Even in 1902 the dockers' federation insisted that a referendum be called before any strike and repeated every eight days. But syndicalist unions, as we have seen, had long preferred oral strike votes, often after the fact, in which an activist minority could prevail. Gradually they too realized that a solidly based strike, one with a chance of winning through a high rate of participation that could be maintained without violence, demanded careful consultation with all potential strikers. Construction workers in Lyons were casting ballots for strikes by 1910. A well-organized campaign for the "English week" in Saint-Quentin in 1912 included careful polling of the workers in each textile factory before a strike was launched. Mine unions polled for strikes in the major basins throughout the period for all officially sponsored campaigns, and these became increasingly formal after 1906, particularly in the syndicalist-led Center (the Saint-Étienne area). These advance votes often prevented strikes in cases where the excitement of a minority had not spread, and they assured extensive participation where the vote was favorable. In February 1912, Saint-Étienne miners voted 4,309 to 620 for a general strike called by the national federation and followed this up by virtually unanimous participation on March 11.[34]

Careful organization continued once a strike was in progress. Syndicalist leaders increased their opposition to artificially prolonged strikes. Alphonse Merrheim, of the metalworkers' federation, noted that many strikes dragged on only because of a clash of *amour-propre* between the strike committee and the employer, not because of any real issues; it was the job of the union to keep demands on the proper plane and to end hopeless strike activity quickly. Merrheim himself closed down several strikes against the will of a minority of activists. In mining as well as metallurgy, union leaders felt free to tell workers that they should not have struck at all and to urge them to quit before they were defeated outright. Unions constantly watched for a level of defections that signalled the imminent collapse of a strike and tried to end the effort cleanly and officially. They clearly contributed to the shortening of the average strike. By 1913, 58% of all strikes lasted five days or less and the average striker spent only ten days on strike, a decline of almost 40% since 1900. Some unions, the miners' federations most notably, were actually calling a term to their strikes in advance.

Precautions against violence increased. In Paris, construction unions hired lawyers to protect their members against arrest, specifically to reduce the temptation to protest violently against police tactics and on behalf of jailed comrades. Thus syndicalist unions increased both their own bureaucracy and their involvement with the existing system in order to avoid needless violence. Demonstrations were still employed to keep workers busy, but leaders learned to distrust them because they could produce unwanted clashes with the police. There was only one placid demonstration in the 1914 Fougères shoe strike, for example, in contrast to the daily marches in 1907. More and more long strikes were maintained by walks in the countryside and picnics in parks, to which wives were carefully invited.[35] Strike committees, especially in Paris, supplemented or even abolished picketing of work sites. Instead they offered daily payments and required each striker to receive a ticket and have it punched daily at a local strike office. Thus violent bands were not needed to enforce adherence to a strike. Again bureaucratic procedures were substituted for direct action. After 1910 many unions were able to promise police authorities a peaceful strike in return for police restraint.[36]

In Paris, strikes on May Day became much calmer, as union leaders were able to control the workers who came to the *bourse du travail* to have their strike cards punched. At most, a few young workers demonstrated and attacked the police. Striking unions still sent workers to visit factory gates and construction sites, but they avoided contact with the police. The 1909 strike by Lille weavers for a local wage rate was completely peaceful; the few demonstrations were orderly. Yet the issue was the same as that which had produced the bloody strikes in Lille and Armentières only six years before.[37] The 1914 strike in Fougères provides another direct contrast. In the lockout of 1906–1907, goaded by employer intransigence, workers were in a violent mood. The daily demonstrations produced numerous clashes with nonstrikers and with the police. In 1914, both sides seemed willing to negotiate and the prefect kept in constant contact with them. There was no violence despite provocations from a yellow union. The strikers set up patrols of older workers to preserve order.[38] Miners in the general strikes of 1913 and 1914 proved that they had learned how to spread a strike without violence. Because of greater union discipline and experience, miners' strikes could be made general in a region in two days instead of the week required in earlier years, and by proclamations alone; the older system of roving bands of strikers was largely abandoned. Without question, union efforts to curb violence bore fruit.

Above all, unions grew more eager to bargain, as they gained experience in conducting agitation. The textile federation which, though not syndicalist, had opposed collective bargaining in 1903 as contrary to class war, had by 1910 turned to vigorous advocacy of negotiation. Syndicalist unions altered their rhetoric less but followed the same course. Hence strikes in which unions were involved resulted in compromise settlements much oftener than did strikes in general, though the number of outright victories was only slightly higher.[39] After 1910 increased bargaining was responsible for the much lower increase in the rate of failure among unionized strikers than among strikers in general. Unions of construction workers, usually syndicalist-led, increased their bargaining efforts most dramatically and conducted the largest number overall, but all unions participated in the movement. If there were few cases in which workers rejected bargaining, there is literally no case in which union leaders did so after 1906, whether with employers or government or both.

Several unions went beyond this, to attempt to incorporate key demands in legislation. As early as 1904 the Paris building trades' unions, syndicalist all, pressed the city to impose an eight-hour day in the next public contracts for subway construction. Some militants attacked this as a betrayal of direct action, but the unions noted that their function was to act for the greatest good of the workers. Syndicalist miners' unions that struck for a better pension law in 1913–1914 followed the same tactic on a national scale.[40]

The changing character of workers' protest was primarily due to increased negotiation. Collective agreements had early precedents: before 1900, scattered groups of printers, weavers, and construction workers had reached negotiated settlements of disputes, particularly in some small provincial centers, and miners in the Nord and Pas-de-Calais gained a truly important contract in the Arras agreements of 1891 covering basic pay and hours of work. Collective bargaining and agreements were rare, however, before 1900; by 1914 they had become common, as di-

rect negotiation replaced conciliation by third parties as a means of settling or preventing conflict.

It is impossible to determine the frequency of collective bargaining or
the number of workers covered by collective agreements by 1914; but
there were hundreds of agreements, affecting hundreds of thousands of
workers. Quarry workers in the Seine-et-Oise won a contract in 1912
that provided a raise and abolition of company canteens and set up a
joint committee to discuss the reduction of hours in winter to prevent
unemployment. Bakers in Bordeaux, wallpaper makers in Toulouse, and
pipe fitters in Saint Cloud gained collective agreements. A contract in
1906 covered 1,900 filemakers in Le Chambon; a settlement in 1905 covered 3,000 porcelain workers in Limoges.[41]

In textiles, a significant minority of the labor force won collective agreements during the period. By 1913, agreements were in effect in at least
twelve cities, usually covering all spinners and weavers if not the whole
working force. As in the first major agreements, signed in Armentières
and Houplines in 1903, textile contracts usually provided a wage rate
and some mechanism by which payments for new articles and for work
on new machinery could be discussed.[42] By 1911 the head of the textile federation, Renard, was hailing the collective contract as "the constitutional regime introduced into the factory." [43]

An even larger number of construction workers won collective agreements. Parisian masons in big firms had a contract after 1909. By 1914
there were at least twenty-five contracts in effect in provincial cities,
with coverage ranging from several thousand masons in Lyons to sev-
enty or eighty roofers or painters in cities like Rennes. A wave of strikes
in Nantes and Le Havre uniformly ended in three-year contracts in
1909–1910; roofers, masons, locksmiths, and painters had them in Nantes,
while painters, stonecutters, masons, roofers, and cabinetmakers were
covered in Le Havre.[44] Most of the contracts followed a similar pattern.
They provided rates for wages and overtime payments and maximum
regular hours according to the season. They usually guaranteed extra
compensation for work on sites at set distances from the city; they often
banned subcontracting. Finally, they almost invariably provided conciliation procedures for subsequent disagreements and at least suggested
a mechanism for renegotiation after the contract period had expired.[45]

By 1909 the leading groups of leatherworkers had won collective contracts. Agreements had been signed in Mazamet, Graulhet, Milhau, Limoges, Grenoble, and Fougères, providing wage rates and sometimes stipulating hours of work.[46] The majority of dockers were covered: by 1910

collective agreements were in effect in Marseilles, Le Havre, Rouen, Sète, Boulogne, and elsewhere, setting pay rates, indemnities in case a job was interrupted, and, usually, hours of work.[47]

Most male printers won agreements through collective bargaining, mainly from 1906 onward. Seventy-three contracts were signed without a strike in 1906, during the campaign for reduction of hours, and over sixty after the strike. Many contracts were signed in later years to regulate wage rates and hours in cities such as Lille, Montpellier, and Paris.[48]

Finally, almost all coal miners were covered by collective contracts throughout the period, for the settlement of the 1902 strike resulted in agreements at all the major basins. The agreements stressed the establishment of rates of pay and bonuses, but even in 1902 the Loire contract promised a fair distribution of work and stipulated that work should end by 3 P.M. each day as a means of assuring that an eight-hour day would be enforced. Later contracts dealt more directly with hours of work and usually required the companies to provide formal pay sheets and to allow worker delegates to transmit complaints and assure the execution of the agreement.[49]

Collective bargaining and contracts thus spread significantly to every major industry except metallurgy. They provided goals for many new groups of strikers, who sought firmer and more general guarantees for their strike demands. The principal goal of most strikes by construction and textile workers by 1910 was a collective contract, and this led to many large strikes with high rates of participation. At the same time, the prospect of fruitful negotiation helped dampen excitement and violence during the strikes. Frustration at their inability to negotiate had long been a primary cause of strikers' violence; this was now often removed. Bargaining usually served to shorten strikes. Most important, collective negotiations tend to prevent strikes altogether. In 1914, Mazamet leatherworkers wanted a raise when their contract was renewed. Their union was anxious for a strike, but the workers believed the time was not right and preferred to negotiate. Discussions with the manufacturers produced a raise, though more modest than the workers had hoped, and a strike was avoided. Armentières weavers were consistently able to renegotiate their contract peacefully, and they usually won a small raise. Waves of excitement often pushed Loire miners close to a strike after 1902, but negotiation prevented all general protest until 1912, when the miners turned their attention toward pressing the government. Loire miners resisted the temptation to join the strikers in the north in 1906, when they won a raise and a small pension for widows by bargaining. Loire unions voted for a strike in 1908, but again bargaining averted it, this time through government mediation; the agreement was renegotiated again in 1910. Many contracts provided specific mechanisms for renegotiation well before the date of expiration. Rouen dockers, for example, were pledged to name delegates to bargain with employers six months before their three-year contract ran out. Other contracts were vaguer and assumed renewal if neither party specifically complained, but there was a presumption that bargaining could occur if necessary.[50] For many workers, the point was clear. As Renard, of the textile federation, noted, peaceful negotiation provided a means to win significant gains "without hostilities, without suffering, without misery uselessly endured."[51] And if a strike was necessary, it more often served as a tool in the bargaining process than as an outlet for anger.

Many collective agreements reduced tension still further by providing arbitration procedures for any grievances during the life of a contract. Early in the period, an outsider was commonly selected for this function. The Armentières contract of 1903 named the highly respected director of the local technical school as the referee for all complaints, and he was able to settle a number of problems about wage rates for new articles. Mining engineers, city architects, and local judges were often chosen for similar purposes. In time, however, mixed committees of employers and workers, either in single companies or in whole cities, replaced or at least supplemented the outsider. Their purpose was to discuss any grievances that arose under the contract and, frequently, to continue negotiations on matters over which no agreement had been reached, such as the number of looms that could be assigned to each worker in Armentières or the hours of work in the mines. In the Mazamet leather industry, a mixed committee set up in 1910 was given the power to decide whether a strike could be called during the three-year life of the contract; any worker with a complaint was to notify his union, which would refer the case to the committee if it felt the grievance was legitimate, and no strike or absence from work was allowed until the committee ruling.[52] After the 1910 railroad strike, local committees were established on all the lines, giving workers "a supple and rapid means to express their desires."[53] It is impossible to determine the number of mixed committees functioning by 1914. In addition to printers, leatherworkers in the major centers normally had them, as did match workers and, somewhat less formally, coal miners. National and local committees were established for merchant seamen in 1909. Textile workers in at least six towns had them, as did many construction workers, including Parisian masons.

Parisian barbers set up committees in several *arrondissements* to enforce the weekly day off.[54] By 1914, many workers and labor leaders
clearly agreed with the sentiment expressed by the head of the typographers' federation fourteen years earlier: "This institution [the mixed
committee] can result immediately in the creation of better relations between employers and workers, by communicating their respective grievances and in consequence avoiding many conflicts by timely explanations; finally, it allows an easier termination of strikes." [55]

The Crisis of Syndicalism

The unions were not entirely successful in moderating strike tactics.
Syndicalists continued to worry about excessive enthusiasm. The metalworkers' federation noted wryly in 1913: "The strike is perhaps a necessary revolutionary exercise, but it should not exclude some reflection
about its consequences." [56] But, as we have seen, tactics did change.
Unions were much more successful in reorienting methods of protest
than in altering the nature of most demands. Despite great pressure by
the unions there was, as we have seen, no real evolution in the pattern
of strike goals in the period. Only the most sophisticated groups, such
as miners and construction workers, learned to seek permanent improvements in their conditions, but they led even more in the adoption of
calm, carefully prepared tactics.

To some observers, the new strike tactics that emerged around 1910
indicated that workers were becoming more conservative.[57] Yet workers'
demands were neither more nor less moderate than before. Both trade
union membership and the strike rate stabilized. The number of strikes
declined slightly but the number of strikers rose somewhat, while outside the formal strike movement many workers pressed successfully for
gains through collective bargaining. Workers had learned to master the
temporary excitement of a strike, to adapt their tactics to their moderation of purpose. They had adjusted their methods to the new environment for labor agitation without great difficulty. The workers' growing
restraint in their methods of striking was a genuine triumph for the labor
unions, including syndicalist unions, in cutting through naive excitement
and disciplining stubborn minorites. Their triumph, however, simply
widened the gap between French workers and theoretical syndicalism.

Small wonder, then, that after 1910 there was growing talk of a crisis
of syndicalism. The crisis resulted, not from a basic change in the
character of French labor, but from the syndicalists' growing understand-

ing of what this character was. Slightly improved material conditions after 1910 and the spread of collective bargaining prevented the development of radically new expectations or grievances. A few groups of workers particularly important to the syndicalists, notably the Parisian construction workers, became more cautious. These changes merely supported the syndicalists' realization that they had never had a chance with French workers. Perceptive leaders li!-e Merrheim yielded to despair.[58]

At the same time many syndicalist leaders were attracted to some of the same accommodations with capitalist society that their constituents were. Syndicalists had never been able to renounce their hope to convert large numbers of workers; after all the general strike depended on mass support. This hope made them prisoners of the workers' own goals, for they had to serve the workers if they were to win them. Some of them were converted to the workers' pragmatism, particularly as the possibility of a general strike grew more obviously remote. The trade union background of the rising generation of C.G.T. leaders, the waning of the old anarchist element, furthered the change. At the top of the C.G.T. there was none of the fire in the new leader, Léon Jouhaux, that there had been in Victor Griffuelhes.

Syndicalism and Protest

As we have seen, syndicalism failed to cause any distinctive features in French workers' protest between 1899 and 1914. The incidence of violence bears no relation to syndicalist influence. Nor does reluctance to bargain (or willingness to bargain) or any particular pattern of demands. Strike demands and tactics varied considerably from one industry or region to the next, but syndicalism was not a factor in the variations.

Two general indices of the character of French strikes need at this point to be put in some perspective. It is true that French strikes were unusually frequent and unusually small in this period, compared to those before and since, and as we have said it could be argued that these characteristics are related to syndicalism. But in a comparative context the significance of the characteristics disappears. France fits fairly neatly in an intermediate position among the European industrial countries in the size and frequency of her strikes before World War I, just as her labor force ranked between the British and the German in the length of its exposure to industrial society. That is, while French strikes were more frequent and included fewer participants than the British, their strikes were less frequent per capita and drew far more participants on the average than German strikes in the same period. The average strike in Germany attracted only 119 participants, almost half the French figure. Yet the German labor movement was furthest of all from syndicalism and was, on the surface, exceedingly well organized. But the German workers themselves were in many ways less disciplined than French and even more likely to strike when suddenly angered, just as they were more fickle in their allegiances to unions. French workers were somewhat better at timing and advance planning. In comparing French and German workers, at least insofar as strike activity is concerned, it is more important to understand their different levels of experience in industrial agitation than to draw on national stereotypes by noting the differences in labor organization or even in economic structure. In a comparative context, the frequency of small strikes in France denotes, not unusual radicalism or pervasive syndicalist influence, but a stage in the development of a more sophisticated labor movement, just as the smallness of the average strike, though again not unusual in context, shows the continued dependence of many strikers on some sort of immediate emotional spur.

Syndicalism cannot be denied a certain negative role. Insofar as it frightened workers away from the unions it not only held French union membership down but reduced its chances of controlling spontaneous protests. The weakness of syndicalist union structure similarly limited discipline. This is doubtless one cause of a few attributes of French strikes, such as the high level of personal-issue strikes, though again there is no direct correlation between this demand and the presence of syndicalist unions, which in turn suggests that other factors, such as the rapid growth of company size, may be more significant. Before 1914 the results of any lag in union discipline were limited because workers in most countries were new to such discipline and more than a bit recalcitrant. This is why so few features of French strikes are distinctive in a comparative context. Insofar as union weakness persisted after World War I, when discipline in other countries improved, the negative legacy of syndicalism may have left a mark on protest in France. This of course requires a study of its own and, in light of the discipline shown in strikes at least from 1936 onward, perhaps a skeptical one.

Three questions remain in this final assessment of syndicalism's impact, two of which have been raised before in a limited way. First, can we dismiss syndicalism so lightly as an important minority movement even if not characteristic of the whole unionized labor force? Second, even if syndicalist theory was unrealistic in the actual strike movement, were syndicalist goals still not held as ideals, as a myth? And finally, does the outburst of protest after World War I not suggest that there was greater radicalism among French workers before 1914 than we have suggested, even if it was largely pent up?

In all industrial countries by 1914, a radical minority of workers were discontented with the evolution of the general labor movement. Some of them were discontented for doctrinal reasons, like the leftist socialists in Germany or some Guesdists in France. Others were angry, like the Welsh miners, because of particular hardship or, in other cases, because of a fear of displacement by machines. We have seen that in many strikes, particularly, in France, before 1910, a radical minority of workers favored goals and tactics that the majority found unrealistic. Some of these workers cooled off later, but many undoubtedly persisted in wanting revolutionary change. Syndicalism could both cause and reflect such sentiments. It had perhaps its deepest hold among workers—like the unionized bakers—who belonged to tiny unions and realized that the apathy or moderation of their fellows made even normal strikes impossible. Syndicalism consoled these workers by pointing to a coming upheaval, and it suggested some violent tactics for small groups right away. Undeniably, syndicalism had a hold on a minority, particularly in Paris. These were people who regularly attended syndicalist meetings, who participated in demonstrations even aside from the excitement of a strike, and who resisted socialist appeals for political participation.

Syndicalism always professed to be the movement of a proletarian vanguard; and historians have always recognized that the majority of French workers were not syndicalist, though they have stressed the importance of the minority. We have suggested that syndicalism failed to develop distinctive strike tactics because it restrained its minority in the interest of wider organizational appeal. But this very fact allows us to go beyond the bland statement that only a minority were syndicalist. The syndicalist minority was very small; many radical workers were not syndicalists; and the radical minority, of whatever stripe, dropped its effective radicalism surprisingly quickly, because major grievances were satisfied or because tactical realities were recognized or because majority sentiment simply smothered it.

We cannot know, of course, exactly how large the syndicalist minority was. A greater knowledge of voting patterns would help determine syndicalist influence. Some Parisian workers resisted Guesdist socialism out of syndicalist convictions—but how many? How many workers abstained from voting on ideological grounds? (For in areas like Roanne and Saint-Étienne syndicalists and anarchists co-operated with socialists and many doubtless voted socialist.) It is clear that, even in Paris, convinced syndicalists were a small minority of active union members. And only a minority of even the more excitable workers were unionized and therefore likely to be syndicalist; in Paris in 1908, that is, in the peak period of agitation by unskilled construction workers, only 40% belonged to a union. The resentment some expressed against being called anarchists suggests a persistent distrust of radical doctrines, even among active strikers.

The syndicalist failure to win some of the potentially most radical workers was remarkable. The ephemeral nature of syndicalist contact with metallurgical workers in Le Creusot and Lorraine can be explained by the vigor of employer resistance. The syndicalists had no time to intervene in the interesting, if rare, revolts in factory towns. But their leadership of quarry workers in the Seine-et-Oise and elsewhere, who had good reason for vigorous protest, did not win many durable converts. And their minor role on the docks was a major handicap. Syndicalism, with its Parisian and artisanal base and its inadequate number of organizers, could not reach out easily. Furthermore, aside from the dockers, the most aggrieved workers were too primitive in their outlook to be quickly converted to any formal labor movement. Metallurgical strikers at Hennebont in 1906, exposed to union agitators for the first time, expressed a common sentiment: "We wondered what the word solidarity meant, which appeared all the time in the letters which were received containing funds." [59] Syndicalist leaders could have only transitory appeal for such workers; so syndicalism, almost inevitably, failed to assemble a significant and persistent minority of the labor force.

Where syndicalism was most fully organized, it had little apparent impact on the workers. The big exception is among construction workers in Paris from 1906 to 1909, but syndicalism merely provided a gloss to the economic factors that were the real cause of agitation. Elsewhere, and in Paris after 1909, construction workers, though led by syndicalists and though concerned about the new machines and the decline of small businesses, did not act in a distinctive or radical manner. Their zeal for collective bargaining is only one example of this. The supposed syndicalism of the miners around Saint-Étienne had little to do with their behavior, save perhaps in their willingness to participate in May Day celebrations. Northern miners, under a reformist union, struck more often, both in general and in partial efforts, and more violently; their union, though eager to preserve good relations with manufacturers and the government, had great difficulty persuading strikers to perform maintenance services during strikes, and maintenance was more often abandoned in the north before 1907 than in other regions where syndicalist unions were in principle reluctant to enforce such work. Who, then, was really a syndicalist? We can never know for sure; but in terms of actual protest activity, it does not seem to matter much.

But what of the myth of syndicalism? Many French workers were certainly exposed to syndicalist ideas through union newspapers, pamphlets, and speeches during strikes and propaganda tours. Surely many workers who realized that radical strikes were not practical at the time (in part because their syndicalist leaders told them so) still had the syndicalist vision of the future. Workers like the Lorraine metallurgists, whose one strike was thoroughly crushed, might have found comfort in the expectation of future upheaval. And of course syndicalist theorists, notably Sorel, began to talk of syndicalism as a myth in part. They recognized that syndicalist tactics, especially the general strike, might never work out, but that the idea of a future upheaval would inspire and educate workers and separate the proletariat from the rest of society. No one can prove that many workers did not harbor radical syndicalist hopes, which they might have admitted were mythical in part. We cannot penetrate so deeply into the minds of workers or any other social group. Certainly a minority may have been persuaded of syndicalism in a theoretical sense, but the behavior of French workers and their expressed goals are hard to equate with any extensive devotion to syndicalist principles. Government agents were not shunned for example, even though the existing government might be bitterly criticized. Lorraine metallurgists, who were unusually repressed and so perhaps susceptible to a radical vision, may have chafed under their employers' authority, but they had outlets in frequent changes of job and (for many) return trips to Italy and in unusually high and rising pay.[60] The most active French strikers had solid but limited expectations, and certainly no interest in strikes for syndicalist principles, while those who did not strike often were either apathetic or largely satisfied. Yet, in this realm where we must speculate without direct evidence, doubts inevitably remain. Syndicalism could not have persisted at all if some groups of workers, particularly in periods of excitement, had not found its rhetoric appealing.

For most active French workers, however, and for some who could not risk direct protest activity, frustrations that could not be expressed in strikes most commonly found a political outlet, in socialist voting. This was another sign of the maturation of the labor movement, and syndicalism played no direct role in it. Many workers had goals or fears or angers that strikes could not serve as a vehicle for. Many were taught by strikes to look to the government, if only the local government, for assistance. On a broader scale, many realized (and ironically some syndicalist leaders encouraged workers to do so) that legislation could accomplish even modest reforms more quickly and generally than strikes could. Some workers, like the textile workers in the north who turned socialist after strikes in the early 1890s, had long combined direct agitation with labor politics. Others were led in this period to political protest by the failure of their strike efforts. Miners in lower Languedoc, for example, had been barred from striking quite early in the period, after an 1897 strike led to massive dismissals and a tightening of police repression. The majority had previously been politically apathetic or simply conservative; but as their unions were defeated, they turned increasingly to socialist politics.[61] Montceau miners followed a similar pattern after their more successful strike efforts in 1899 and 1901, though they remained in the syndicalist miners' federation. Strikes were not the only factor in the growing trend to socialism and the conversion of workers was far from complete, but the trend was clear. For some workers, like those in textiles who suffered miserable pay but could launch only primitive strikes, socialism expressed deep-seated grievance. For others, like the many miners both in the north and around Saint-Étienne who supported reformist socialists, socialism was another way to seek solid but limited gains. Happily we do not have to judge the revolutionary content of socialism in this study. It clearly varied from one type of socialism and one type of worker to the next. The effectively reformist evolution of French socialism and the mood of workers revealed in strikes make it probable that socialism had little revolutionary content up to 1914, even of a mythic sort.[62] In any event, whether for social upheaval or for piecemeal gains, workers had learned that political action was the wave of the future, and this, too, made syndicalism increasingly irrelevant.

Doubtless some workers voted socialist while maintaining syndicalist ideals; some of the Saint-Étienne miners might be a case in point. Historians should not require more consistent behavior or thought of workers than of anyone else. Again, the issue of syndicalism as a cherished myth cannot entirely be disposed of. Yet syndicalism was far less appropriate than socialism as a revolutionary religion that could be maintained along with pragmatic behavior. There are two points here. First, although syndicalism easily rivaled socialism in its passionate denunciations of the existing order and its preoccupation with tactics, it did not have a clear enough vision of the future or of the historical past to constitute a complete theology. Some workers might have been satisfied by the discussions of tactics, but most, of that minority that sought a labor religion, required more. In addition, syndicalism did not provide the institutions and related ritual that socialism usually did, to maintain the faithful in good cheer and apart from the established order. Syndicalists sometimes used a black flag at meetings, but this was not distinctively syndicalist; they used songs, notably the "Internationale" and the "Carmagnole," but they were not syndicalism's own. The ritual apparatus was simply not there. This meant that the convinced syndicalist was more alone, more alienated, than the convinced socialist. For socialist ritual and institutions provided, in France as elsewhere, a certain social integration even if apart from the more general society. But for the syndicalist to stand thus alone, he had to have an almost overwhelming anger against the existing order. Few French workers had this anger.

What, then, of the outburst of strikes and political protest after World War I? [63] Syndicalism still existed, though by this time the C.G.T. leadership was clearly reformist. Some older syndicalist leaders and even new ones, like the railroad leader Monmousseau, who had not begun to participate in antimilitarist meetings until 1913, played a role in the unprecedented wave of agitation. Some of these leaders helped form the new communist party and union movement. Beyond this, workers in a few areas, like Saint-Étienne and Saint-Nazaire, maintained or renewed some attachment to revolutionary syndicalism. But the revolutionary vanguard at this time came from different types of workers—such as metallurgical workers around Paris, whose numbers had advanced as a result of war industries; and from others, such as newly articulate peasants and school teachers. The new radicalism was not the same as the old, and it took different, nonsyndicalist forms. The war and subsequent economic difficulties, plus the Russian revolution, may have raised workers' expectations considerably. Indeed, the war must be seen as a crucial turning-point if many French workers were then revolutionary, for this had not been the case before. Strike goals became more political, the tactics were directed increasingly against the government. New types of workers awakened, like the 10,000 seamstresses who struck in 1919. This was not simply a prewar revolutionary mentality in new guise.

On the other hand, the postwar explosion was only temporary, and outside of politics it left few traces. After 1920 and until 1936 French workers still sought modest goals with modest strikes. There was an important revolutionary minority in this period, but it still had only limited effect. It is not clear that a decisive change in the expectations of French workers occurred until the great depression and a second war took their toll. This, of course, goes well beyond the present study. For our purposes, it seems safe to assert that insofar as labor protest rose after World War I, it was because of new factors rather than a persistence of older trends, and even then the changes in the character of the French working classes may not have been decisive.

Motivation of Syndicalists and of Workers

Why did syndicalism, a revolutionary philosophy, take any hold in a nonrevolutionary environment such as that of French labor before 1914? Aside from syndicalism's possible service to a small minority of workers and its appeal as a myth, the principal explanation must be this: the causes that operated on labor leaders differed considerably from those that affected most ordinary workers in this period, though some of these leaders themselves came from the ranks of workers, particularly artisans. Syndicalism as a doctrine had deep roots in French intellectual and political tradition, from the Revolution and thinkers like Proudhon if not from an older, rationalist individualism. The syndicalist leaders were open to doctrine and avid for political ideals. They had inherited the revolutionaries' mantle, they felt the tragedy of the Commune, and they read or read about Proudhon and Blanqui. Syndicalism served also as a vehicle for a real revulsion against socialist dogmatism and reformism. For the syndicalist leaders were deeply hostile to socialism, and syndicalism thus served as an outlet for revolutionary strivings that a minority of labor leaders in most countries developed after the character of prewar socialism became clear. In other words, the motive forces for the leaders were intellectual and political.

Doctrinal traditions had less impact on French workers than on their leaders, and the socialist movement, where it was known, was not unduly reformist. Economic factors played the key role in shaping protest behavior, and they were not at this time conducive to radicalism. Most workers had not read Proudhon. Most workers were not significantly moved by the great revolutionary tradition.[64] It is absurd to assume that they were shaped by formal ideas and remote political events. The very real causes of syndicalism, then, had little bearing on the labor force. We have seen one illustration of the gap between the causes of workers' actions and those of the leaders' rhetoric in the incidence of violence in strikes. There were good reasons, in the traditions of Blanqui for example, for syndicalists to advocate violence. But with very few exceptions the patterns of actual violence were linked, not to such traditions or to the urgings of syndicalists themselves, but to the age, type of work, and frequency of unemployment of the workers. This idea of two strands of causes in the labor movement, one impelling leaders and one motivating most active workers, demands serious consideration by labor historians. It means, quite obviously, that a contact between leaders and workers is not necessarily a conversion, as is often assumed. It means that much of the labor history of this period, not only in France, must be seen as an effort by leaders to impart their motivations to the workers. The French syndicalists failed.

One result of this duality was that, for many workers, the kind of labor organization that was accepted was almost accidental. It depended on what leader or organization was available in a crisis. Hence the northern miners, who began an important new surge of protest in the late 1880s, found reformist socialist leadership available and they maintained their attachment to it throughout our period, even though they were demonstrably angrier than most syndicalist groups. Correspondingly, many workers later joined syndicalist unions because syndicalist leaders were there to answer appeals for help or, in some cases, because these leaders had aroused hopes in the first place. The reasons for a particular movement being available and for workers wanting to belong to a movement were not the same.

This accidental element will distress those who insist on seeing syndicalism as a logical expression of French workers' character, or German socialism as a logical expression of German workers' character. I do not claim that there was no correspondence at all. We have seen that construction workers had some good reasons to pick syndicalism, especially in Paris. But no particular difference in operative causes explains why some miners or textile workers were in syndicalist unions while others were not; this was a function of what leaders were present when the leadership was needed. On the whole, syndicalism owed its main contacts with the workers simply to its existence and its ability to give guidance in organization, not to its program.

But workers were not passive tools. They might seize on outside leadership because it was available, but they were not content to follow it blindly. In Germany, socialism and the workers interacted, with the result that while socialism became more pragmatic the workers became less individualistic, more disciplined. Socialist methods and goals made some sense, in short. This was not the case with French syndicalism. It answered, at best, the enthusiasm of the moment. It could not radicalize immediate goals and probably had only limited success in shaping ultimate hopes. It was not attuned to the industrial age, and French workers, though moderate, were. Syndicalism was paralyzed outside of the realm of theory, where it showed some continued vitality.

Syndicalism persevered for a decade or two. Its advocates were vigorous. They produced distinctive and abundant rhetoric. They fit most of the stereotypes about French workers and French industry. Yet they did not characterize French labor in their heyday and they did not set an enduring trend. Their image lives in the minds of those historians who wish that workers had been what they were not. Surely serious students of working-class history can leave them there.

4 Conclusion

Realization of syndicalism's insignificance in France is vital for an understanding of the impact of labor protest before 1914. This is another advantage in cutting through the rhetoric of protest. French society at the turn of the century must be rated unusually stable because it was not wildly misled by flaming speeches and congress resolutions.

As we have seen, innumerable French workers were so shocked by syndicalist pronouncements that they rejected the labor movement altogether. Syndicalist slogans played a role in antagonizing public opinion, though the same antagonism developed in other industrial countries where syndicalism was not involved. Employers found it easy to use syndicalism as an argument against the labor movement. A member of the Lille Chamber of Commerce, speaking in 1909, expressed a common argument: "Today work ceases abruptly, without reason; it is not resumed even if the employers grant the formulated demands. One feels the secret intervention of a foreign will which pursues a strategic goal by mobilizing its troops, by preparing them to obey any surprise order." [1] The government also was clearly offended by syndicalism. Radical republicans in parliament turned against working-class protest in large part because of the syndicalists' verbal insurrectionism.[2] It is possible that parliamentary efforts at social reform, seemingly prepared by the Radicals' program and their co-operation with socialists before 1905, were stalled in the crucial years 1906–1909 because of the fear roused by syndicalists' agitation and the socialists' insistence on defending the syndicalists at the expense of collaboration with the Radicals.[3] This interruption of social legislation, which contrasts with developments in other industrial countries, may have been the most important result of syndicalism in France. In sum, syndicalism helped produce a reaction to direct labor protest that would have developed anyway, to judge by the similar trends in Britain and Germany. At most it advanced the process by a few years. New police policies emerged after 1906 instead of after 1910 as was the case elsewhere. At the same time the reaction was not so severe in France.

For neither the government nor the employers took syndicalism too seriously. Syndicalism created a much milder sense of crisis than occurred in Britain after 1910, under the impact of the huge strike wave.[4] The outlook and behavior of French workers did not interfere with or threaten the functioning of the Third Republic, and its leaders knew this. We must balance a few tough speeches and police incursions against normal policy, which did not become more repressive. Employers, similarly, handled workers' demands with some conciliation. They were not rigorously antagonistic because they knew that syndicalism did not describe what their workers wanted. There was no significant movement for severe antistrike legislation such as arose in Germany immediately before the war. Syndicalism failed, then, thoroughly to *épater les bourgeois*.

As we enlarge our understanding of protest movements, we can use them to assess not only the groups from which protest springs but also the nature and solidity of the broader society.

The removal of syndicalism as a major variable in French labor history certainly facilitates the further study of industrial protest itself. French workers can be compared more readily with workers in other industrialized countries where syndicalism did not arise. Syndicalism had a genuine appeal in newly industrializing areas, particularly in Italy and Catalonia.[5] Here workers were protesting not simply specific issues of hours and wages but the nature of the system itself. Hence their strike rates were much higher than those in any of the industrialized countries, the strikes themselves were more violent, and direct action had political (or antipolitical) goals. By the same token to ascribe importance to syndicalism is to complicate the interpretation of the stages of French protest. It encourages false analogies with much less developed countries.[6] It would mean that French workers somehow yielded to a rather primitive protest structure despite their unrivaled experience in the art and the various signs of modernization in their protest after 1848. Historians cannot insist on invariably neat patterns and I have no wish to ignore the distinctive aspects of French labor protest, in which syndicalism played some role. But we can justifiably seek a broader conceptual framework.

At the same time, some of the reasons for syndicalism's failure in France indicate the complexity of the evolution of labor protest. Syndicalism could be a roaring success where, as in Catalonia, ex-peasants, already aggrieved by rural hardship and injustice, were newly exposed to industry and looked to an idealized past. French workers, even the new ones, were beyond this stage. But their freedom from traditional canons of protest varied greatly. The recrudescence of market riots suggests the fragility of generalizations about a decisively new pattern of protest even in a relatively advanced stage of industrialization. The actual patterns of strike activity show that large categories of French workers were in a transitional rather than definitely "modern" phase of protest. The designation "modern" or "industrial" is usually based on assumptions that labor movements can be taken at face value. French syndicalists in practice urged progressive protest on the labor force; they did not dwell on the anti-industrial implications of their doctrine. French workers were not ready to respond fully. Nor of course did they reject syndicalism because its organizational structure was too weak. They could have been led to accept more developed protest organizations, but, like workers in Germany at the same time, they did not spontaneously demand such organizations. They relied heavily on small-group loyalties and most of them still argued in terms of the past. The Lille workers who demanded equal pay for equal work used phrasing that recalls earlier popular resentments of unfairness, for example. We too easily assume that workers are capable of a rapid transition to high collective expectations.[7] In fact this conversion, at least in Europe, was extremely complex, particularly for factory workers as opposed to artisans. Well after 1914 radical protest continued to depend on catastrophe, just as the absence of severe economic setbacks explains the moderation of French workers' goals in the two decades before 1914. The persistence of modest expectations explains much of the complexity of the relationship between formal labor movements, including syndicalism, and even the angriest workers.

French workers had substantially adjusted to an industrial society. Their grievances, solid as they were, were developed within this framework. Syndicalism in practice, as we have seen, like most labor movements in industrial countries, encouraged further integration by preaching collective discipline, negotiation, and improvements in wages and hours. The existence of syndicalism has fed, and its importance been exaggerated by, the idea of a distinctive French lag in industrialization and indeed a positive resistance to it. Without question, French manufacturing was incompletely industrialized, but where was the process complete? Certainly not in Germany, the favorite standard of comparison. German big business was bigger, to be sure. But there were at least two industrial economies in Germany, and the more populous sector was

unusually backward.[8] French textiles and leather goods companies were
more concentrated and technically advanced.[9] In printing 50% of the
French labor force worked in units with over fifty employees in 1906,
whereas Germany had only 44% in this category a year later; and auto-
matic compositor machines were introduced far more rapidly in
France.[10] Even within France the common generalizations about a craft-
based economy have ignored the average size of companies in heavy
industry and the vast numbers of workers employed.[11] There is no need
to dispute a French industrial lag so long as lag is understood to be a
difference of degree and not of kind.[12] French workers cannot be compre-
hended otherwise.

Syndicalism would have caught on in France had there been more
workers like the shoe repairmen in Paris cited earlier who wished to
protest modern industrial forms. It was an ideal vehicle for a truly
alienated worker. Students of French labor generally assume that French
workers, because of unusual individualism, were unusually aware of the
alienation of factory life.[13] In fact, syndicalism was largely irrelevant
precisely because the workers capable of protest, led in fact by the most
skilled, accepted the industrial system. This is all the more notable given
the rapid extension of mechanization and the other trappings of industrialization after 1895.

There were far fewer signs of yearning for rural life or the traditional
crafts among the French than among the Germans, because a recog-
nizably industrial, urban labor force had existed longer in France. The
extent of small-group loyalty evidenced in French strike patterns belies
any facile notions about French individualism or a growing isolation of
the individual worker from his fellows amid the new industrial forms.
Most important, French workers' high and persistent interest in wage
demands reflects a remarkably positive attitude toward industrialization.[14]
Divisions of outlook within the labor force complicate any interpretation.
Textile workers were troubled by the new, larger looms, but they were
more preoccupied with maintaining their wage rates. The concern about
wages was, even in textiles, a concern for the individual reward which
could be obtained from industry. Furthermore, the groups of workers
who led in developing progressive material demands were among those
most exposed to important changes in technology and business organization. They were willing to accept their new conditions in return for
higher earnings and some reduction in the hours of work. Workers such
as printers and shoe mounters struck with unusual frequency, which reflected their edginess, but they demanded compensation for change, not

a return to the past. Metallurgical workers, in most countries the first to accept technical change, did not need to protest frequently because their rising earnings made new technology acceptable. In various ways, French workers made the basic bargain that industrialization requires of its servants.

Large questions remain. What of the workers who did not protest? Was there an alienation among workers who accepted more routinized work methods in return for higher earnings that did not directly find its way into protest? The vast group of transitional workers, epitomized by the labor force in textiles, who accepted an industrial structure without having developed progressive material demands invites particular study. What of the individual adjustments that workers made or failed to make through mobility and changes in family structure that formal protest did not necessarily express at all? The central problem of working-class history is to interpret reactions to fundamental economic change by the group most directly exposed to it in industrialization. Most labor historians have been too busy documenting the internal politics of the labor movement to ask workers themselves what was going on. We must ask them, even to find out what the labor movement meant.

Appendices

Appendix A: Real Wages and Strikes

Virtually all historical studies of prices and wages in this period contend that real wages rose, though at a slower pace than before, until 1910, and then dropped under the impact of a massive rise in prices; and recently an attractive theory has been advanced to associate the trend in strikes with this evolution. It may seem bold to challenge such a well-established view, though it might be noted that some contemporary economists expressed doubts about the rise of real wages before 1910.[1] Certainly the points at issue require discussion; indeed my principal hope is to open renewed inquiry, for if the precise pattern of real wages in a fourteen-year period is of rather specialized interest, the related question of why workers struck and what they wanted is basic to any understanding of labor history.

Professor Jean Lhomme has recently rephrased the usual presentation of real wage trends.[2] He indicates a 10% improvement in real wages between 1900 and 1909, then a 7% decline by 1913. This conforms to the interpretations of government statisticians in the period (not surprisingly, since their figures have been the basis of all later studies) and of Jürgen Kuczynski, who normally seeks to paint as black a picture as possible.

My criticism of these interpretations, advanced with real humility since I lack the credentials and probably the depth of interest of many previous students in the history of wages for its own sake, has several bases. First, the government tables minimized real price increases: figures in government reports themselves are frequently higher than the index numbers the final tables record. Second, and most important, the government tables list prices of goods consumed by workers, but without weighting them for the actual importance of the items in working-class budgets. It is unfortunately true that we lack as ample studies of worker budgets in this period as exist for Britain and for Germany. But two detailed studies under the direction of Maurice Halbwachs and an earlier inquiry by the British Board of Trade, all of which are mutually consistent, give some basis for a more accurate approach.[3] The approach has to be attempted. One of the principal elements of the presumed decline in prices between 1900 and 1906, for example, was the reduction in wine taxes. If the consumption of wine is made as extensive as that of bread or meat, the result is indeed close to the government's picture; but this is obviously nonsense. Further, and this is the third basis for my approach, indications from Halbwachs and a few other scattered sources point to a deterioration in actual consumption levels, particularly of meat, by 1910. This obviously needs more investigation; it might be added that historians of wages have too often simplified their task by sticking to wage and price figures alone, without trying to determine what actual consumption rates were. The increased reliance on the earnings of women and children in this period also suggests a deterioration in real wages by 1910. Finally, the usual interpretation of wage patterns simply does not coincide with what workers themselves were saying in strikes and other protests. It is true that the greatest explosion against price rises came with the market riots of 1910–1911. But strikers had been mentioning such increases for at least five years before this. Obviously they may have been confused or they may have lied; but again wage historians have made their work too easy and their accounts too abstract by ignoring this sort of subjective evidence.

Of course there are large areas of uncertainty in the study of wages, even aside from the possible unreliability of the figures available. We know too little about rates of unemployment. Professor Lhomme specifically discounts the possibility of considering these rates at all, and perhaps he is right. Yet if we neglect this subject, what do we know of workers' conditions? The standard interpretation of real wages reveals a peak in 1909; but in that year, union figures suggest an unemployment percentage of almost 8%. Clearly average conditions had worsened, not improved, and any interpretation of strikes in the next few years must take this into account. Similarly my impression that real wages rose a bit after 1911 may result in part from the apparent fact that unemployment fell well below the 1900–1910 levels. Our information about unemployment is admittedly quite uncertain, but the factor must be considered.

Similarly the historian of wage patterns should ideally know the changes in supplementary resources for working-class families, from gardens to paying lodgers to working wives and children. This information is very badly developed for France, though census figures offer some assistance. Finally the whole discussion of wage trends may be distorted with regard to the actual living standards of the average worker, which is presumably what all of us are trying to get at, by mobility within the work force. That is, a decline on the wage charts of the real pay of machinists' assistants may be almost meaningless if machinists' assistants were rising to semiskilled jobs with higher pay and their place was being taken by unskilled workers—women for example—who previously earned still lower wages. On the basis of this sort of mobility a historian of British wages has asserted, without any effort at proof unfortunately, that British workers' pay was improving throughout this period despite a decline on paper in real wages in the average job category.[4] I cannot pretend that I have as yet been able to take all these factors, particularly the last one, into account for France, but it seems important to raise the questions at any rate.

Money wages rose for almost every major group in the labor force during the period as a whole. Between 1901 and 1906 alone, average pay for manufacturing work rose over 4%, from 4.03 francs a day to 4.20 francs. After 1906, in most cases, the gains were even more substantial. Miners' wages, which had risen only 2% by 1906, after falling between 1903 and 1905, had risen a full 17% over 1900 levels by 1914. There was a 3% improvement between 1909 and 1911 alone, from 4.97 francs to 5.12 francs a day. Metallurgists' pay advanced in a similar fashion. There was a significant decline in 1902, but by 1911 a 9% gain over 1900. Around Longwy and in the booming northeast generally, metallurgists and iron miners gained over 20% by 1910. Metalworkers' incomes rose also. The wages of blacksmiths and locksmiths increased 17% in Paris between 1901 and 1911, 11% outside of Paris.[5]

Pay for construction workers and other groups of artisans rose rapidly, though on the whole the principal gains occurred after 1906. In Paris, the wages of masons, housepainters, and ditchdiggers stagnated between 1901 and 1906, while those of carpenters actually fell; but there were major gains in the next years. Ditchdiggers, despite their lack of skill, made the most rapid strides. In Paris between 1901 and 1911 their pay rose by a full third, from .60 to .80 francs an hour, while in the provinces it increased 18%, to an average of .39 francs an hour. Masons also made a significant advance, by 19% in Paris, to .95 francs an hour, and by 11% in the provinces, to .49 francs. Painters lagged a bit, their wages rising by 7% in Paris and by 11% in the provinces; and provincial carpenters had won only a 6% gain by 1911. Still, there was no category of construction workers in any major region which suffered from declining pay; and for the group as a whole the gain was clearly over 10%.[6]

Typographers had made no gains in Paris by 1911, maintaining their .80-franc-an-hour level, but they were granted raises averaging 12% in the provinces. Stevedores' earnings advanced up to 30% in the major ports.

In fact, the only major group that did not share fully in the general advance was in the textile industry. Weavers' pay rose a healthy 29% between 1901 and 1911 according to the general national statistics, though even then the rate was still a low .35 francs per hour. A more detailed view casts some doubt on these figures. Weavers' pay rose in Lille, in Marseilles, in Mazamet, in Castres, and in many other centers; in Roanne it increased also, but by only 3%. And in several leading textile cities it declined. It fell in Rheims from .40 francs an hour in 1900 to .32 in 1911; in Tourcoing from .40 to .35; in Rouen from .37 to .30; in Saint-Quentin from .27 to .23. Among weavers, at least, the picture of a significant gain must be severely modified, as a result of the sluggishness of the industry.[7] More important, most of the increase in hourly rates was due to the 16% reduction in hours of work between 1900 and 1904; this limited the real increase in money wages considerably.

But on the whole, for the leading categories of manufacturing and transport labor, the government's estimate of a 10% rise in money wages by 1910 seems to be modest; and for groups such as miners, at least, there were continued gains until the war. There was a decline or stagnation in money wages between 1901 and 1905 in many cases, but this was more than made up for later on. For rough calculation, a rise of 12% by 1910 can be assumed, though the uneven distribution of the gain among the major industries should not be forgotten.

In 1907, it was estimated that the average working-class family devoted 70.8% of its budget to food, 10.5% to rent, with the rest going for clothing, dues, education, and recreation. Workers with above-average earnings could scale down the percentages devoted to food and housing, though they typically increased the absolute expenditures particularly on food. Within the food category, approximately 17.8% went for bread, 25.9% for meat, 7.5% for milk, 12.4% for drink. These are of course rough estimates at best, and the balance of the expenditures altered somewhat during the period; but they may serve in a general calculation.[8]

Until 1911 at least, prices rose in almost every category of working-class expenditure. The cost of cloth and probably of clothing went up. Heating costs rose. Coal prices fell 14% between 1901 and 1905, but by 1909 they were 2% above the 1900 level. Rents rose rapidly. The average annual rental for cheap housing in Paris was 167 francs in 1900, 200 francs in 1911, an increase of 20%; this alone represented a 2.1% rise in the total cost of living for workers. In the provinces the rent increase was more modest, 7.4% between 1900 and 1910, but it was still burdensome. Union dues certainly rose, probably by 300%, though workers were notoriously unwilling to pay them. Insofar as can be determined, the non-food items in working-class budgets all increased significantly in cost, and most of the cost increases were fairly steady.[9]

There were several relatively minor food items whose prices remained steady in the period, notably coffee, butter, and sugar. The cost of wine declined until 1907, because of the tax cut, by about 10%. But all other items in the budget rose in cost, usually rapidly. The price of potatoes increased 75% between 1900 and 1909; the price of eggs rose 10%. Between 1900 and 1908 the price of milk rose up to 25% in many cities. Meat costs rose considerably. The price of beef mounted 33% in France as a whole between 1900 and 1909. Pork was up by more than 30% in Paris between 1900 and 1910, while veal prices rose 20%; increases of similar magnitude occurred in other French cities. And bread prices rose almost as much in France as a whole, though they were modest in a few major centers such as Saint-Étienne. There was a steady increase in the price of wheat, 30% between 1900 and 1909, and bread prices generally followed this at a somewhat slower pace. For the whole country the price rise was 23% between 1900 and 1909. In Paris, two kilograms of bread cost .62 francs in 1900, .77 in 1910—an increase of 24%.[10]

The price increases of bread, milk, and meats, given the proportion of workers' income spent on them, added 12.5% to the total cost of living by 1910. The decline in wine prices was probably fully compensated by the increases in potatoes, eggs, and other items. When combined with the rise in rents, the only other major item for which a precise measurement is available, rising prices caused an increase of over 14% in cost of living for Parisian workers by 1910 and a rise of over 13% in the provinces. Other major expenses were increasing also.

The result, in terms of real wages, seems clear. Average metallurgical pay did not increase as fast as prices did before 1910, though there were important regional exceptions. Miners' pay barely met the price increase, and between 1901 and 1906 lagged behind it; the same is true for all construction workers before 1906 and for many categories thereafter. The average hourly pay of textile workers rose sufficiently, according to general evidence; but this was not the case in several of the most prominent centers. Given the reduction in the hours of work, it is clear that real wages fell in French textile manufacturing as a whole. For the working class generally, again by inexact calculations, real wages stagnated or fell during the first decade of the century.

After 1911, real wages probably improved, for, at least in food, price levels stabilized and money wages continued to rise slightly. Even the rent increase seems to have moderated. Meat prices rose but less rapidly; and workers spent a smaller proportion of their budget on meats, no doubt because of the cost. Instead of 25.9% of the food budget, as in 1907, meats commanded only 21.9% in 1913. On the other hand, bread prices definitely stabilized and workers were buying more bread than before (devoting 24.3% of their budgets to it, instead of 17.8% as in 1907). The combination of price changes and new buying habits led to a definite stabilization of food costs between 1911 and 1913. During these years, an index of thirteen food prices, including all the major items, revealed almost complete stability in France as a whole. The leading industrial districts, the north and the east, actually experienced a decline of less than 1%, while the west was stable and prices rose about 5% in the southeast and south.[11]

The evolution of working-class consumption standards after 1900 confirms the general impression of deterioration of conditions before 1910 and gives some weight to the idea of a slight improvement at the very end of the period. The decline of meat consumption was steady, but most rapid before 1909. In Paris during the whole period, per capita meat consumption fell from 62 kilograms a year to 54.5 kilograms. Milk consumption declined. Bread consumption rose very slightly, though as we have seen, the portion of the budget spent on bread increased because of the price rise. The consumption of items whose price fell or remained stable increased definitely. Per capita wine consumption rose 11% between 1900 and 1910, but then fell slightly. The later decline reflected the increase in wine prices but also, perhaps, the new price stability of other items of consumption. Per capita consumption of sugar and coffee in the working class rose steadily, and the rate of increase mounted after 1911. Sugar consumption, for example, increased by 24% between 1900 and 1910, then rose 23% during the next three years. The consumption of tobacco increased. In general, a reshuffling of food purchases occurred because of the variations in the patterns of major food prices. But because few workers won any real increases in their purchasing power between 1900 and 1910, the quality of the working-class diet declined.[12]

Outside the category of food, where evidence is scantier, similar readjustments seem to have occurred. Compared to other groups in the population, such as white-collar employees, blue-collar workers did not show great interest in improved housing. Higher-paid workers devoted most of their extra income to food, clothing, and entertainment; the percentage of their budget assigned to rent was actually lower than that of their poorer colleagues. This relative unconcern about housing was encouraged by the rent rise; and the percentage of budgets devoted to rent actually fell between 1907 and 1914 from 10.5% to 8%. As a result of this, there may have been a positive deterioration in housing for workers. On the other hand, per capita expenditures on clothing increased, particularly after 1911. So did payment of union dues and, probably, expenditures on recreation.[13]

The improvement of workers' living standards from 1911 to 1914, after a decade of mild decline, was fed by the slight rise in real wages, the decline in unemployment, and also, in all probability, by the increased dependence on the earnings of children. One investigator noted an increase in average family earnings among urban workers from 1,700 francs in 1907 to 1,969 francs in 1913–1914. He noted also that disparities within the working class had increased: 36% instead of 34.9% of workers' families earned less than 1,000 francs, while 36% instead of 25% earned over 2,000. And, in 1907, 76% of the income had come from the father, 11.7% from the mother, 9.9% from the children, and 2.5% from other sources. By 1914 the father contributed only 73%, the mother only 5.4%, but the children 18.5%.[14]

The standard interpretation of the evolution of real wages is certainly compatible with an understanding of the outburst of workers' protest after 1900, and recent studies have embellished the compatibility. The standard argument is that before 1910 the increase in the strike rate was due to disappointed expectations despite the presumed improvement in real pay. The improvement was not as rapid as in previous decades. After 1905 the rise in prices perhaps created a sense of deterioration even where none existed. Above all, workers simply wanted more than they were getting; some might even invoke the fact that profits were rising more rapidly than wages.

But why, then, did the strike rate stabilize, even decline slightly, when according to the conventional picture real wages deteriorated under the impact of the price rise from 1910 onward? For this we now have a specific theory, one with the real merit of trying to determine what workers were prepared to ask for.[15] Workers find it difficult to strike during an inflationary period. They sense price increases only vaguely and slowly, because they do not keep budgets. Even when they realize that prices are rising they cannot see the utility of strikes to counteract the rise, since the strike is a weapon against employers and the most visible villain in inflation is the merchant. (Hence, when prices rose so extensively in 1910–1911 that workers could not fail to notice, the most direct response was market riots.) Only perhaps after World War II have French workers gained the sophistication that allows them to strike with increasing intensity when prices are advancing.

This theory makes a great deal of sense, and it of course reconciles the strike rate with the standard interpretation of real wages after 1910. I agree fully that workers were often slow to realize the impact of inflation, because of inadequate budget-keeping and because the whole phenomenon was rather new in this period. Many were undoubtedly disarmed by rising money wages even when these were inadequate. But I must dissent from the theory as a whole. Obviously, if my judgment of the trend of real wages is accurate I have to dissent, for in my view the rise in the strike rate before 1911 was in considerable measure due to deterioration in real wages, and the stabilization of the strike rate after 1911 was the result of the stabilization of the standard of living.

I also find it difficult to reconcile a statement that French workers were too inexperienced to use strikes to maintain their real wage in an inflation with the belief that they were fully capable of asking for positive improvements in their wages before inflation hit. Agreeing that inflation was novel and required some adjustment of thinking, I contend that the conversion to truly progressive wage demands was far more difficult than to strike for maintenance of the real wage. Indeed, inflation aided this conversion by teaching workers that unprecedented increases in money wages were essential. Furthermore, why, if workers protested against inflation in 1910–1911 (and the rise in the strike rate in 1910 must have been due at least in part to inflation, along with the market riots), did they forget about inflation after 1911? The explanation must be that inflation has to be truly massive to be noticed. But the price rise between 1911 and 1912 was precisely the same as that between 1909 and 1910, even according to the standard interpretation of Lhomme and others, yet the strike rate remained stable and there were no riots; and throughout these years there was plenty of propaganda about "la vie chère" (which began, it must be noted, well before 1910 though it increased thereafter) to help teach workers to fight inflation. I think French workers had increasingly learned to combat inflation with strikes between 1905 and 1910; that the outburst in 1910–1911 was the culmination of this fight; that after 1911 the fight waned because real wages were advancing slightly at last. There is no question but that French workers talked about price rises well before 1910. The view that they could not perceive inflation rests in large measure on the labor historian's old trick of not consulting evidence from workers themselves.

British workers were certainly capable of using the strike to attack inflation after 1910. Inflation was the major cause of the massive outburst of those years. It was to be sure a serious and therefore particularly noticeable inflation. And it could be argued that British workers, with greater industrial experience, were more alert to inflation than French workers were. I would argue precisely the reverse. French workers realized that inflation was occurring sooner than British workers did and well before 1910. There are a number of probable reasons for this. French workers spent more on food, which was the category in which prices rose most rapidly. Before this time and afterwards, their strikes reveal unusual interest in wage questions. Why this is so, is open to question: the traditional insistence by French employers that the wage was all they owed their workers (in contrast to most other continental employers) is the best explanation. But in any event the French workers' preoccupation with wages helped them realize the impact of price increases. Finally, if few working-class families kept budgets, working-class wives in France were definitely better organized housekeepers than their counterparts in Britain. The many studies of British housewives reveal an unparalleled sloppiness in accounts and a long period in which the women simply did not know that prices were rising. French women gave the message to their husbands much more quickly.

For the outstanding fact is that strikers from at least 1905 onward invoked inflation as a major reason for their demands. Sometimes they did so at the suggestion of their union, but often the claim was spontaneous. They continued to invoke inflation after 1911, because many categories of workers had still failed to make good their pre-1911 losses; typically they mentioned a whole period, such as 1900–1912, rather than the preceding year or two when they talked about price rises. The claims of workers themselves and the fact that they made these claims well before 1910 cannot be ignored. The theory that inflation reduced strikes on the assumption that real wages began to fall only in 1910 will not hold up. For the years after 1911 the theory must also stress a reduction in striking, when stabilization of the strike rate (both in number of strikes and in number of strikers) is a far more accurate description. And it must ignore the intense interest on the part of workers in improving their wages collectively but without strikes after 1910. The spread of collective negotiations in these years, which almost invariably produced modest but important raises, made strikes unnecessary for many workers but did not indicate a lack of desire to maintain real wages or to improve them. Even if I am wrong about real wage trends and inflation was overwhelming after 1911, it would be hard to argue that workers were paralyzed in their response, if negotiations are considered along with strikes.

Everywhere in industrial Europe there was a coincidence between the rise in strike rates and inflation in this period. In countries where real wages increased despite inflation, like Germany, strike rates advanced but did not attain the levels of France or Britain (there were more strikes, but far fewer strikers). It required a real deterioration in conditions to produce a massive strike wave such as that in Britain after 1910. Despite the conventional interpretations of French wage patterns, I see no reason to hold that France was an exception to the continuing relationship between deteriorating conditions and an upsurge of protest. France developed high levels of agitation between 1900 and 1911 because real wages were falling and workers knew it. Strikes leveled off after 1911 as real wages stabilized. They remained as high as they did after 1911 in part because workers were still trying to catch up—the unskilled in most regions, for example, were slower than the rest to realize inflation was occurring—and because expectations were rising among certain categories of workers. Because price inflation did outstrip earnings before 1911 and because French workers were in an unusually good position to realize this, the decade was crucial in teaching growing numbers of workers to insist on steady increases in money wages. This set the tone for the firm if calm bargaining of the last prewar years. At the same time, the disaster had not been sufficiently massive to convert French labor as a whole to a new level of demand. Even World War I did not effect a durable conversion, for what is involved is an extraordinarily difficult human change.

Appendix B: Statistical Characteristics of Strikes and Their Evolution

The following figures are drawn from STAT; totals have been computed by the author for manufacturing and transport strikes alone.

TABLE I: NUMBER OF STRIKES AND STRIKERS PER YEAR

Year	Industrial and transport strikes	Industrial and transport strikers
1899	749	182,649
1900	808	225,364
1901	532	171,746
1902	558	209,214
1903	586	117,822
1904	892	206,888
1905	791	222,281
1906	1,319	509,274
1907	1,131	201,105
1908	969	89,991
1909	1,060	184,592
1910	1,292	296,935
1911	1,281	205,172
1912	1,045	244,690
1913	965	215,759

TABLE II: PERCENTAGE OF STRIKES WITH UNION MEMBERS INVOLVED

1899	55.4	1907	75.4
1900	59.8	1908	74.7
1901	65.2	1909	77.3
1902	64.5	1910	78.5
1903	67.1	1911	75.2
1904	73.7	1912	74.1
1905	82.0	1913	71.7
1906	78.2		

Overall Average: 72.8

TABLE III: ANNUAL NUMBER OF STRIKERS IN THE AVERAGE STRIKE, 1899–1913

1899	243	1907	178
1900	341	1908	93
1901	341	1909	174
1902	375	1910	230
1903	201	1911	160
1904	232	1912	234
1905	281	1913	224
1906	386		

Overall average: 239

TABLE IV: ANNUAL PERCENTAGE OF ONE-COMPANY STRIKES, 1899–1913

1899	77.7	1907	71.0
1900	67.9	1908	80.4
1901	70.3	1909	76.8
1902	82.6	1910	74.4
1903	78.9	1911	67.5
1904	74.2	1912	76.5
1905	72.5	1913	78.4
1906	65.0		

Overall average: 73.7

TABLE V: ANNUAL AVERAGE PERCENTAGE OF THE RELEVANT WORK FORCE
INVOLVED IN THE AVERAGE STRIKE, 1899–1913

1899	80	1907	57
1900	84	1908	40
1901	84	1909	55
1902	90	1910	70
1903	88	1911	50
1904	86	1912	40
1905	84	1913	60
1906	74		

Overall average: 65

TABLE VI: LEADING STRIKE DEMANDS, 1899–1913 *

Demand †	No. of strikes	Percent of all † strikes	Percent won	Percent lost	Percent compromised
A. Wages					
For salary increase	7,714	55.9	17.5	36.4	46.1
Against pay cut	576	4.2	28.3	35.9	35.7
For an increase in piece rate	273	2.0	24.9	27.8	47.2
Against piece rate reduction	129	.93	20.9	45.0	34.1
Total	8,692	63.0			
B. Worker dignity and participation					
To rehire dismissed workers (or directors)	1,726	12.5	14.5	55.1	30.4
To fire directors (or workers)	1,634	11.8	17.2	52.0	30.7
Union recognition	145	1.0	13.1	42.4	44.5
Solidarity	346	2.5	19.6	34.8	45.6
Total	3,851	27.8			

* In all charts, rounding of percentages sometimes produces totals of 99.9 or 100.1

† Total percentages of demands, in this and subsequent tables, add up to over 100, because of strikes in which multiple demands were involved.

TABLE VI (*Continued*)

Demand	No. of strikes	Percent of all strikes	Percent won	Percent lost	Percent compromised
C. Length and pace of work					
Hours ‡	2,138	15.5	15.9	36.4	50.6
End piece rate	270	2.0	13.0	38.1	49.0
Work rules	504	3.6	15.4	37.5	47.0
Fines	324	2.3	15.1	39.2	45.6
Work conditions	116	.84	25.9	37.0	37.0
Total	3,352	24.0			
D. Legislation	46	.33	13.0	17.4	69.6
Totals	13,805		19.8	41.6	38.6

‡ 144 of the strikes over hours of work protested an increase in hours; 1,369 insisted on a positive reduction.

TABLE VII: CHARACTERISTICS OF STRIKES FOR THE MAJOR DEMANDS

A. Duration

Demand	Percent 1–5 days	Percent 6–10 days	Percent 10–30 days	Percent 31 or more days
Pay increase	46.1	18.5	22.4	13.0
Against pay cut	50.4	17.5	19.2	12.9
Rehire workers, etc.	54.0	16.4	18.3	11.3
Fire directors, etc.	54.7	16.9	17.8	10.6
Union recognition	26.7	16.7	29.9	26.7
Hours	39.9	16.3	26.8	17.0
Rules	51.2	15.8	27.0	16.0
Overall averages	51.1	17.2	19.9	11.7

TABLE VII (*Continued*)

B. Number of Companies

Demand	Percent 1 company	Percent more than one
Pay increase	65.5	34.5
Against pay cut	84.5	15.4
Rehire workers, etc.	91.6	8.4
Fire directors, etc.	91.5	8.5
Union recognition	59.6	40.4
Hours	50.6	49.4
Rules	81.2	18.8
Fines	90.1	9.8
Work conditions	76.7	23.3
Overall averages	73.7	26.3

C. Percentage of Strikers from Relevant Work Group *

Demand	1–50% of Work Group	50–100% of Work Group
Pay increase	13.7	86.2
Against pay cut	16.4	83.5
Rehire workers, etc.	20.3	79.7
Fire directors, etc.	15.2	84.8
Union recognition	16.5	83.5
Hours	14.0	86.0
Rules	15.4	84.6
Fines	18.2	81.8
Work conditions	14.2	85.8
Overall averages	16.1	83.9

* The government statisticians tried to define "potential strikers," that is, workers affected by the issues involved, and compared this with actual strikers. Criteria for this sort of judgment were admittedly uncertain, particularly in strikes that involved less or more than one company.

TABLE VIII: INCIDENCE OF DEMANDS IN THE

Demand	Trans-portation	Mining	Metal-lurgy	Stone—earth (ceramics, glass, jewelry, etc.)	Carriage making, fine-wood products, wood-working	Con-struction (masonry, ditch-digging, roofing, etc.)
Pay rise	51.5	48.2	44.8	53.6	49.5	22.3
Against cut	2.0	4.1	4.1	5.8	7.6	2.1
Rehire workers	14.5	16.8	18.0	15.6	11.8	9.0
Fire directors	9.4	13.9	19.8	9.9	12.8	9.3
Union recognition	1.2	1.4	2.1	.37	1.2	.62
Hours	14.2	19.6	15.8	11.1	17.0	17.4
Rules	4.2	5.8	4.6	4.5	3.7	1.2
Fines	1.2	6.9	2.2	2.2	1.8	.24
Work conditions	.9	.9	.9	.56	.76	.6
Solidarity	5.5	4.3	2.1	1.9	1.5	1.1
Against piece rate	.7	1.4	3.4	3.2	6.7	1.5
Legislation	0	.9	.5	.2	.8	.8
All pay demands	54.6	52.7	52.0	63.3	62.0	75.6
All pace and length of work demands	14.9	21.0	19.2	14.3	23.7	18.9
All conditions of work demands (in-cluding hours and pace)	21.2	34.6	26.9	21.6	30.0	20.9
All demands relating to dignity and worker voice	30.6	36.4	42.0	27.8	27.3	20.0

Major Industries, 1899–1913, in Percentages

Bâtiment (carpentering, furniture making)	Leather	Textiles	Paper and printing	Chemicals	Food processing	Quarries
82.5	50.7	50.6	41.2	55.9	64.3	61.9
1.3	6.2	6.5	4.3	2.4	2.2	7.9
2.9	14.0	11.0	16.1	15.3	8.1	11.3
6.5	13.7	11.2	13.8	11.5	8.1	13.0
8.3	.6	.6	.09	1.9	3.0	.8
21.4	9.3	9.0	36.1	11.1	25.9	15.1
1.1	6.8	4.1	3.8	5.0	3.4	2.5
.89	2.7	4.4	2.1	3.1	2.7	2.1
0	1.3	.9	1.0	1.4	1.5	1.3
2.2	2.8	1.5	2.1	7.7	2.5	5.4
4.2	1.0	1.2	1.6	.7	.25	3.3
.7	0	.1	0	0	.25	.42
84.0	61.5	64.5	46.9	58.5	67.2	70.2
25.6	10.3	10.2	37.8	11.8	26.2	18.4
27.6	21.1	18.6	44.7	21.3	33.8	24.3
19.9	31.1	24.3	32.1	36.4	19.9	30.4

TABLE IX: EVOLUTION OF INCIDENCE OF MAJOR DEMANDS, IN PERCENTAGES

	1899	1900	1901	1902	1903	1904	1905	1906	1907	1908	1909	1910	1911	1912	1913
Pay rise	50.7	59.8	50.9	43.1	48.6	43.3	43.4	58.8	62.3	53.9	53.6	61.4	60.1	57.6	59.3
Against cut	9.2	6.6	8.1	12.1	7.7	6.1	3.3	2.5	2.1	3.5	2.7	1.2	2.1	3.4	2.8
Rehire workers	7.7	9.1	9.6	7.6	10.7	11.8	15.0	9.9	13.8	14.2	19.5	13.5	14.3	14.2	11.0
Fire directors	10.4	10.3	15.0	13.3	11.4	12.0	16.1	10.6	11.9	10.8	12.1	13.0	10.3	13.0	12.2
Union recognition	.41	0	.38	.75	.17	.8	1.14	1.9	2.1	.95	2.1	1.6	.86	.86	.21
Hours	15.0	13.6	15.2	17.2	10.9	23.3	16.1	34.0	12.2	13.8	12.5	11.6	12.3	10.2	9.3
Rules	3.8	7.3	11.1	4.7	5.8	3.8	4.8	2.6	3.3	3.2	2.9	2.9	1.4	2.6	2.4
Fines	1.6	2.4	3.0	3.5	4.4	3.4	4.3	3.6	2.6	1.5	1.2	1.2	1.6	1.2	1.8
Work Conditions *	0	0	0	0	0	0	0	1.6	3.1	1.1	1.4	.55	1.5	.48	.42
Solidarity	1.5	.75	1.3	6.2	6.1	6.4	0	3.2	1.4	1.4	2.0	1.3	2.3	1.1	.62
Against piece rate *	0	0	0	0	0	0	5.3	5.5	3.1	1.7	2.9	2.3	3.4	2.0	2.4
For piece rate rise	7.1	.87	.94	3.7	2.0	9.6	1.8	1.2	1.4	.95	.66	.55	.94	.86	.42
Against piece rate cut	1.1	.25	2.3	2.2	1.5	1.0	1.8	.61	.45	.32	.85	1.2	.78	.1	1.1
Legislation	.41	.10	2.4	.93	.85	1.3	1.4	0	0	0	0	.08	0	?	? †
All pay demands	68.1	67.5	62.2	61.1	59.8	60.0	50.3	63.1	66.2	58.6	57.8	64.3	63.9	62.1	63.6
All pace and length of work demands	15.0	13.6	15.2	17.2	10.9	23.3	16.1	39.5	13.6	15.5	13.4	13.9	15.7	12.2	11.7
All conditions of work demands (incl. hours and pace)	20.4	23.3	29.3	25.4	21.1	30.5	25.2	47.3	22.6	21.3	18.9	18.5	20.2	16.5	16.3
All demands relating to dignity and worker voice	20.0	20.0	26.3	27.9	28.4	31.0	37.5	25.6	29.2	27.4	35.7	29.4	27.8	29.2	24.0

* Because of changes in categories used to describe strikes, demands later listed as related to work conditions or opposition to the piece rate were not so described before 1906, so the lack of figures for 1899–1905 should not be taken as literally accurate; there were, however, few such demands before about 1906.

† Government figures give zero for both these years, but major mining strikes were conducted over legislation.

TABLE X: DURATION OF STRIKES

Years	Per-cent 1–5 days	Per-cent 6–10 days	Per-cent 11–15 days	Per-cent 16–20 days	Per-cent 21–5 days	Per-cent 26–30 days	Per-cent 31+ days	Average days per striker
1899	54.8	18.8	9.5	5.5	1.7	1.5	8.2	—
1900	53.0	16.7	10.5	5.4	3.0	2.0	9.4	16.5
1901	53.7	17.9	7.1	6.0	3.4	2.2	9.7	16.8
1902	49.5	19.0	10.0	4.5	3.6	2.0	11.4	21.9
1903	44.6	17.0	8.8	4.5	4.5	2.6	18.0	19.8
1904	50.6	16.7	9.9	5.7	4.0	1.9	11.1	14.6
1905	50.7	16.2	9.9	4.9	3.9	2.5	11.9	15.5
1906	45.7	17.9	9.9	6.8	3.9	3.2	12.5	21.6
1907	52.6	17.9	9.2	4.6	3.1	2.6	10.0	18.0
1908	55.4	15.6	7.5	3.3	2.2	2.5	13.5	17.7
1909	52.4	16.5	9.1	4.9	3.4	2.9	10.7	21.3
1910	47.2	18.3	9.1	5.4	3.1	3.0	13.8	17.2
1911	47.1	19.4	9.6	4.4	4.4	2.6	12.5	16.2
1912	53.8	17.0	8.2	4.6	2.9	2.1	11.5	9.0
1913	57.6	14.0	7.9	4.8	3.3	1.8	10.7	10.1
Overall average	51.1	17.2	9.1	5.0	3.4	2.4	11.7	16.9

TABLE XI: STRIKE DURATION AND RESULTS, 1899–1913, IN PERCENTAGES

Duration	Won	Lost	Compromised
1–5 days	25.0	43.8	31.2
6–10 days	17.4	39.4	43.2
11–15 days	14.6	38.9	46.5
16–20 days	12.9	39.8	47.3
21–25 days	13.0	38.6	48.4
26–30 days	16.7	41.5	41.8
31 days +	10.2	38.6	51.1

TABLE XII: EVOLUTION OF STRIKE RESULTS, 1899–1913,
IN PERCENTAGES

Year	Won	Lost	Compromised
1899	23.3	38.7	38.0
1900	21.9	38.8	39.3
1901	22.6	41.3	36.1
1902	23.7	38.1	38.2
1903	19.4	36.0	44.5
1904	23.6	36.3	40.2
1905	22.3	34.5	43.1
1906	20.0	36.6	43.4
1907	19.5	41.0	39.5
1908	17.0	50.9	32.1
1909	20.3	40.5	39.2
1910	19.7	40.5	39.8
1911	16.7	46.9	36.4
1912	16.5	48.7	34.7
1913	16.4	48.3	35.3
Overall average	19.8	41.6	38.6

TABLE XIII: EVOLUTION OF THE RATE OF STRIKE FAILURES FOR
5 COMMON DEMANDS, 1900–1913, IN PERCENTAGES

Year	Pay raise	Hours of work	Rehire workers, etc.	Fire directors, etc.	Rules
1900	36.0	25.5	53.4	38.5	29.0
1901	38.4	46.9	37.2	51.2	33.9
1902	38.1	20.7	41.5	57.8	32.0
1903	30.2	34.9	58.7	38.8	32.3
1904	32.5	27.0	51.5	41.9	42.4
1905	34.5	21.3	51.7	52.8	31.6
1906	30.7	35.3	46.9	48.2	41.2
1907	36.6	34.8	48.0	47.4	35.1
1908	45.1	49.2	60.7	59.8	40.0
1909	34.9	28.6	64.6	48.4	21.7
1910	33.7	30.7	51.4	56.6	40.5
1911	37.9	36.1	61.2	65.1	27.8
1912	42.2	46.7	63.5	59.6	40.7
1913	43.4	43.8	58.5	52.5	60.9
Overall average, 1900–1913	36.35	33.4	55.1	52.0	37.5

TABLE XIV: UNIONS' ROLE

A. Annual Percentages of Strikes Involving Direct Negotiation
between Unions and Employers.

1903	6.0	1909	9.3
1904	6.0	1910	3.5
1905	12.4	1911	3.1
1906	11.2	1912	2.1
1907	8.0	1913	4.3
1908	9.5		

B. Rates of Strike Failure, in Percentages.

Year	Overall	In strikes with union workers involved
1899	38.7	35.3
1900	38.8	35.8
1901	41.3	38.3
1902	38.1	33.2
1903	36.0	36.4
1904	36.3	34.7
1905	34.5	32.3
1906	36.6	35.4
1907	41.0	39.1
1908	50.9	49.3
1909	40.5	38.7
1910	40.5	40.1
1911	46.9	45.9
1912	48.7	47.3
1913	48.3	44.6

TABLE XV: CHARACTERISTICS OF STRIKES IN

	Total strikes	Percent won	Percent lost	Percent compro-mised	Percent of strikes with union workers involved	Percent duration: 1–15 days
Food	410	16.7	47.3	36.0	67.5	61.7
Paper-printing	610	20.4	45.6	34.0	85.0	46.1
Bâtiment *	449	20.6	30.0	49.4	82.5	36.6
Construction †	2,896	19.6	44.1	36.3	64.5	55.6
Woodworking ‡	659	23.4	39.5	37.1	78.8	39.6
Stone-earth §	543	18.4	38.4	43.2	73.7	42.7
Quarries	245	13.4	41.0	45.6	67.8	40.8
Chemicals	423	19.4	41.7	38.8	64.0	62.2
Leather	678	25.3	35.6	39.1	86.3	41.3
Textiles	3,035	21.2	39.8	39.0	66.2	48.3
Transport	1,691	21.9	39.4	38.7	78.5	66.6
Mines	558	12.8	39.9	47.3	71.5	55.2
Metals	1,803	16.2	47.5	36.3	82.4	44.6
Total, all industries	13,968	19.8	41.6	38.6	72.8	51.1

* Carpenters, cabinetmakers.
† Masons, ditchdiggers, roofers, etc.
‡ Carriagemakers, makers of fine wood products.
§ Ceramics, glass, jewels.

THE MAJOR INDUSTRIAL CATEGORIES, 1899–1913

Percent duration: 6–10 days	Percent duration: 11–31 days	Percent duration: 31+ days	Percent more than one company	Percent of strikes with over 75% of relevant work group participating	Average number of strikers	Percent of negotiation and conciliation efforts
17.1	18.3	2.9	50.2	67.7	100.1	16.0
17.4	23.8	12.8	26.1	59.7	119.4	17.0
17.6	26.4	19.4	71.7	79.4	116.1	29.0
15.0	18.1	11.3	37.4	74.6	178.9	27.0
18.7	25.3	16.3	33.5	72.4	144.9	19.0
17.8	18.7	20.8	20.1	73.2	137.8	17.0
23.3	22.0	13.9	39.6	83.8	153.0	16.0
18.9	15.0	3.8	6.4	64.2	207.8	9.0
19.6	25.3	13.8	19.0	72.3	143.2	23.0
18.8	21.6	11.3	11.8	72.0	206.1	12.0
16.3	12.7	4.4	31.0	67.9	335.3	12.0
13.1	15.9	15.8	8.2	60.8	1220.9	18.0
17.7	24.1	13.6	16.4	68.6	197.5	15.0
17.2	19.9	11.7	25.5	70.8	200.2	16.0

TABLE XVI: ANNUAL RATE OF STRIKES AND

Year	Food strikes	Strikers	Paper-printing strikes	Strikers	Bâti-ment strikes	Strikers
1899	19	1,704	36	4,400	19	2,043
1900	39	4,227	22	1,220	24	2,342
1901	22	1,746	12	987	13	497
1902	9	1,008	29	1,273	8	358
1903	21	1,664	24	1,205	10	1,052
1904	37	3,866	32	5,352	14	1,033
1905	29	2,877	32	2,891	27	2,417
1906	54	4,673	186	36,069	32	11,925
1907	27	3,684	38	5,761	37	5,827
1908	14	1,420	38	1,843	29	1,690
1909	23	1,483	32	2,468	31	2,247
1910	26	4,045	43	3,551	54	9,280
1911	36	2,803	36	2,334	71	4,676
1912	17	909	13	1,037	37	2,730
1913	36	4,941	37	2,449	43	3,891
Change 1899–1905 to 1907–1913 *	+2%	+13%	+27%	+12%	+171%	+211%

Year	Chem-icals strikes	Strikers	Leather-working strikes	Strikers	Textile strikes	Strikers
1899	13	5,809	13	1,405	221	42,490
1900	27	10,624	47	11,911	228	124,439
1901	17	4,140	40	4,206	113	14,827
1902	43	16,646	14	1,592	176	36,033
1903	7	717	40	5,546	235	77,014
1904	23	10,891	41	7,304	217	74,751
1905	35	6,703	98	16,324	148	26,277
1906	32	5,348	65	14,092	225	52,572
1907	35	5,908	52	4,915	225	28,985
1908	24	1,407	37	3,214	133	11,857
1909	20	1,924	48	9,132	206	34,731
1910	46	5,427	41	2,818	341	47,533
1911	38	3,529	53	7,092	190	17,036
1912	38	5,987	53	4,438	167	13,920
1913	25	2,721	37	3,093	211	22,906
Change 1899–1905 to 1907–1913 *	+37%	−52%	+10%	−28%	+3%	−62%

* This figure conveys something of the trend of strike rates in each category by dividing 1899–1914 into two segments of equal length (each with two recession years) and omitting 1906 as an atypical peak.

STRIKERS IN THE MAJOR INDUSTRIAL CATEGORIES

Construction strikes	Strikers	Woodworking strikes	Strikers	Stone-earth strikes	Strikers	Quarries strikes	Strikers
95	15,744	43	2,949	35	6,808	22	4,883
106	11,185	33	4,148	28	3,107	0	0
73	8,765	39	3,485	20	6,815	11	2,683
64	4,350	22	1,170	18	6,162	3	172
42	4,033	26	1,980	21	1,087	9	1,385
105	14,061	40	3,237	53	3,715	0	0
100	84,695	44	13,797	34	13,089	20	4,736
222	63,268	69	26,484	56	5,401	17	2,772
269	35,225	53	3,402	44	4,531	16	2,800
388	34,498	35	2,291	56	5,035	34	4,707
256	39,971	29	2,181	29	5,346	19	1,338
327	67,475	54	9,808	26	2,337	25	3,918
363	84,173	71	7,010	54	6,881	43	4,505
274	27,695	52	5,767	40	3,148	26	3,575
215	20,905	49	7,830	29	1,361	0	0
+258%	+116%	+39%	+24%	+33%	−29%	+151%	+50%

Transport strikes	Strikers	Mines strikes	Strikers	Metals strikes	Strikers
46	8,354	35	33,265	152	52,795
113	42,870	53	44,247	88	15,044
88	95,782	20	19,454	68	8,359
37	10,848	46	119,747	89	9,855
61	11,586	23	2,452	92	8,101
190	62,804	36	8,021	104	11,853
85	13,910	19	5,165	121	29,340
89	17,279	71	179,045	201	90,344
160	69,355	41	10,045	134	20,667
82	8,848	35	7,805	69	5,376
247	66,895	30	8,393	90	8,483
124	96,526	23	11,607	101	32,610
140	36,995	27	8,765	159	20,373
117	20,107	39	133,347	174	22,030
112	34,920	60	89,887	111	20,855
+73%	+39%	+10%	+12%	+25%	−4%

Notes

Introduction

1. In this book the term "syndicalism" is used for what might more precisely be called "revolutionary syndicalism," that is, that advocacy of transferring control of production to workers' unions and abolishing formal government by means of a revolutionary general strike. Syndicalism can of course refer also to a corporate theory of government or to a system of economic organization independent of revolutionary means of achievement. I use the term in preference to "revolutionary syndicalism" simply to avoid cumbersomeness in a label that must often be repeated in the text.

2. As I must often refer to the frequency with which historians have summed up French labor as syndicalist, insofar as it was active at all outside of politics, a brief bibliographical note is necessary here. Almost all the surveys of the French union movement relate not only union developments but also strike activity to the syndicalist theme. Non- or antisyndicalists are ignored or at best reduced to a tiny voice amid the syndicalist roar. Two recent studies show how easy it is to classify French labor before 1914 in syndicalist terms: R. Goetz-Girey, *Le Mouvement des grèves en France, 1919–1962* (Paris, 1965), pp. 30–33, and *passim;* and Robert Wohl, *French Communism in the Making* (Stanford, 1966). W. A. McConagha, *The Development of the Labor Movement in Great Britain, France, and Germany* (Chapel Hill, 1942) is a useful presentation of the conventional view. In Paul Louis, *Histoire du mouvement syndical en France* (Vol. I, Paris, 1947), still the best detailed summary for this period, syndicalism maintains its sway in French unionism with only minor challenge until 1910 at least; little else seems to merit discussion. And so it goes, in specific studies of French labor and in passing references.

3. E. P. Thompson, for example, uncritically accepts the representativeness of radical spokesmen, whether from the working class or not, in *The Making of the English Working Class* (New York, 1963), pp. 451 ff.

4. In fairness, it has been recognized that the C.G.T. was a minority movement and that many workers stayed away from unions precisely because they were afraid of syndicalism. But this still leaves the impression that the dynamic minority—and most active labor movements anywhere at this time were the work of a minority—was syndicalist. See Val R. Lorwin, "Reflections on the History of the French and American Labor Movements," *Journal of Economic History* (1957), p. 25.

5. See Goetz-Girey, *Le Mouvement des grèves, passim.*

6. Ted Gurr, *The Condition of Civil Violence: First Tests of a Causal Model* (Center of International Studies, Princeton University, *Research Monograph* No. 28) (Princeton, 1967); Ronald G. Ridker, "Discontent and Economic Growth," *Economic Development and Cultural Change* (1962–1963), pp. 1–15.

7. Charles Tilly, "Collective Violence in European Perspective," in Hugh Davis Graham and Ted Gurr (eds.), *Violence in America: Historical and Comparative Perspectives* (Washington, 1969), pp. 7 ff.

8. On national character and French labor, see Lorwin, "Reflections," *passim;* and Reina Uirtanen, "French National Character in the Twentieth Century," in "National Character in the Perspective of the Social Sciences," *Annals of the American Academy of Political and Social Science* (1967), p. 82. I have reviewed the national character approach for several European countries in "National Character and European Labor History," *Journal of Social History* (1970), pp. 95 ff.

9. For a good summary statement, see Ephraim H. Mizruchi, "Alienation and Anomie: Theoretical and Empirical Perspectives," in *The New Sociology* ed. I. L. Horowitz (New York, 1964), pp. 253–67; see also S. Parker and R. J. Kleiner, *Mental Illness in the Urban Negro Community* (Glencoe, Ill., 1966).

10. These figures are computed from STAT. The official statistics are inaccurate even in the gross tabulation of numbers of strikes. Charles Tilly and Edward Shorter have used newspaper accounts as a check against these statistics and find that roughly 10% of all strikes, including some large ones, were unrecorded by the government. The official figures which this study uses give an adequate idea of trends but they leave a margin of error.

11. See J. Juilliard, "Le Syndicalisme révolutionnaire et les grèves," *Mouvement social* (1968), pp. 55–69. This brief study indicates, at long last, some interest in the behavior of syndicalists as labor leaders, in addition to repeating their pronouncements. It errs only in attributing far too much influence to the syndicalists. For a study of the largely abortive syndicalist efforts to educate the workers before 1902, see Alan B. Spitzer, "Anarchy and Culture: Fernand Pelloutier and the Dilemma of Revolutionary Syndicalism," *International Review of Social History* (1963), pp. 379–88.

Chapter 1

1. This was true at least after anarchism failed in France; many anarchists, of course, turned directly to syndicalism. See Jean Maitron, *Histoire du mouvement anarchiste en France (1880–1914)* (Paris, 1951).

2. Some French workers, especially in metalwork, were discontented with the voluntary plans; they believed that their employers forced them into the plans and then deducted too much from their pay. But this was only indirectly expressed as a grievance against the government. French workers' vigorous defense of their money wages in this period suggests that a fuller contributory social insurance scheme might have been resented. This is not to deny, of course, that the political representatives of French labor pressed for such legislation. French workers, lacking the experience of social insurance that German workers had and the pragmatic political sense (and leadership) of the British, may have been slow to support an active demand for insurance. In contrast with the British, they also lacked the acute problems of unemployment that helped motivate such a demand.

3. René Waldeck-Rousseau, *Questions sociales* (Paris, 1900), p. 113; AD Vosges 8 M 95[1], government circular of Nov. 1904 describing the conditions in which meetings should be banned.

4. APS B/a 1360, on the railroad strike; AN F[22]234, a summary of existing procedures on handling strikes with an eye to revision of the law (1912).

5. APS B/a 1353 (on the 1907 bakers' strike) and 1363, report of Oct. 13, 1910, on crimes and arrests in the railroad strike; AN F[7]13923 (on the railroad strike) and F[22]167 (on arrests in 1905 strikes); Pierre Tesche, "La Grève des boutonniers de l'Oise," *La Revue syndicaliste* (1909), p. 149.

6. AD Nord M625/74. The strike in La Gorgue-Estaires was neither violent nor serious; the police measures were prompted by the severe strike wave in the region earlier in the year. Yet the measures, if unusual, were not unique in mild strikes, since strike waves often called forth generalizable fears. On police procedures see also Paul Louis, *Histoire du mouvement syndical en France* (Paris, 1947), I, 281; A. Willaert, "La Grève du bâtiment de Dunkerque," *La Vie ouvrière* (1910), p. 100; AD Isère 166M/9, on police tactics in Grenoble in 1906; Alphonse Merrheim, "Le Mouvement ouvrier dans les bassins de Longwy," *Mouvement socialiste* (1905), p. 473; APS B/a 1382, on police measures in the masons' general strike of 1909.

7. On reactions to police at strike meetings: APS B/a 1362, surveillance during 1910; G. Airelle, "Les Evènements de Raon-l'Étape," *Mouvement socialiste* (1908), p. 101; AN F[7]13774, report on Couéron metallurgy strike; AN 48 AQ 3402 (archives of the Compagnie du chemin de fer du Nord), report of Oct. 14, 1910.

8. See Claude Willard, *Les Guesdistes* (Paris, 1965).

9. *Bulletin de la statistique générale de la France* (1911–1913), *passim.*

Unemployment among unionized British workers averaged 4.3% between 1894 and 1909, a figure actually lower than in France. I believe that Britain had higher rates overall, however, when the largely nonunion unskilled are considered. See *Labour Gazette* (June 1911); Edward G. Howarth and Mona Wilson, *West Ham* (London, 1907).

10. Ministère du travail et de la prévoyance sociale, *Résultats statistiques du recensement général de la population effectué le 4 mars 1906* (Paris, 1909), I, 159; Ministère du travail et de la prévoyance sociale, *Résultats statistiques du recensement général de la population effectué le 5 mars 1911* (Paris, 1913), I, 19–20; Jean Lescure, *Hausses et baisses des prix de longue durée* (Paris, 1933), p. 64.

11. The usual qualifications must be made before embarking on an effort to determine the movement of real wages. The statistical materials are incomplete. Price figures are amply available for food and rent, but not for other major items in workers' budgets. For prices and even more for wages, there is only sketchy information after 1911. Wages varied greatly by industry and region; and even for the same job in the same region, pay might vary by 20% from company to company. In any given year, bread prices differed by as much as 100% from one department to the next, and there was divergence from town to town within a department. Averages are greatly suspect. For wages, particularly, they are deceptive. Daily wage averages can be fairly well established, confirmed by several government sources and by some union reports; but they say nothing about how many days a year a worker was able to earn. They say nothing also about increments to income from company benefit programs. The major railroad companies each spent several million francs a year on bonuses, pensions, schools, and direct aid for poorly paid categories; the benefits could add over two hundred francs to the individual's annual income. Comparable programs existed in the larger metallurgical and mining concerns. At best, amid these various uncertainties, probabilities can be established; exactitude is impossible. R. B. Forrester, *The Cotton Industry in France* (Manchester, 1921), p. 85; BOT (1902), pp. 434 ff.; Clément-Eugène Louis, *Cantonnier-poseur de voie du chemin du Nord* (Paris, 1904), pp. 486 and 491. For a fuller discussion of wage patterns and their relation to strikes see Appendix A, which more fully presents the conventional view and its refutation.

12. *Bulletin de la statistique générale de la France* (1911), p. 54; Albert Aftalion, "Le Salaire réel et sa nouvelle orientation," *Revue d'économie politique* (1912), pp. 546 ff.

13. Jürgen Kuczynski, *Die Geschichte der Lage der Arbeiter in Frankreich von 1700 bis in die Gegenwart* (Berlin, 1949), p. 256; Jean Marczewski, *Introduction à l'histoire quantitative* (Geneva, 1965), pp. 164 ff.

14. Albert Aftalion, *Les Crises périodiques de surproduction* (Paris, 1913), I, 195; Jean Bouvier, François Furet, and Marcel Gillet, *Le Mouvement du profit en France au XIXᵉ siècle* (Paris, 1965), pp. 107, 113, 175.

15. Ministère du commerce, de l'industrie, des postes et des télégraphes: office du travail, *Bordereaux des salaires pour diverse catégories d'ouvriers en 1900 et 1901* (Paris, 1902), p. x; Kuczynski, *Geschichte der Lage*, p. 254; *Bulletin de la statistique générale de la France* (1913), p. 359; François Simiand, *Le Salaire, l'évolution sociale, et la monnaie* (Paris, 1932), III, Table I; Ministère du travail et de la prévoyance sociale: direction du travail, *Salaires et durée du travail* (Paris, 1907), p. 297; Fédération nationale des travailleurs de l'industrie du bâtiment, *Annuaire* (Paris, 1911), pp. 184 ff.

16. See Appendix A. M. L. Dugé de Bernonville, "Enquête sur les conditions de la vie ouvrière et rurale en France en 1913–1914," *Bulletin de la statistique générale de la France* (1911), p. 73, and (1913), pp. 190 and 198; *Bulletin de la statistique générale de la France* (1911), pp. 37 ff.; Émile Levasseur, *Questions ouvrières et industrielles en France sous la troisième république* (Paris, 1907), p. 507; Ministère du travail, *Salaires et coût*, pp. 46, 53, 386, and 505; Maurice Halbwachs, "Revenus et dépenses de ménages des travailleurs. Une enquête officielle d'avant-guerre," *Revue d'économie politique* (Jan.–Feb. 1921), pp. 55–57.

17. German workers, for example, had a distinctly inferior diet. Their meat consumption per person averaged 30% less than that in France. They consumed poorer quality starches also, and almost certainly faced more crowded housing conditions. A rather close comparison, which admittedly falls short of statistical certainty, is possible through three publications of the British Board of Trade: *Report of an Enquiry into Working Class Rents, Housing and Retail Prices in the Principal Industrial Towns of France* (London, 1909); *Report of an Enquiry into Working Class Rents, Housing and Retail Prices in the Principal Industrial Towns of Belgium* (London, 1910); *Report of an Enquiry into Working Class Rents, Housing and Retail Prices in the Principal Industrial Towns of the German Empire* (London, 1908). My argument here is that one must look to the deterioration of conditions, not to a comparison of absolute levels of conditions, to explain radical protest in this period, at least in the industrial areas of Europe. German workers immediately after World War I showed that they could respond to increased hardship by intense protest, though of course it did not take syndicalist forms.

18. Ministère du travail, *Résultats statistiques du recensement . . . 1906*, II, 10–15; Ministère du travail, *Résultats statistiques du recensement . . . 1911*, I, 20.

19. *Le Réveil du Nord*, Oct. 6, 1902.

20. AD Ille-et-Vilaine 60 Mb/8, report of Nov. 1912, on importation of strike breakers to Fougères; AD Pas-de-Calais M1788, on strike breakers on the Dunkerque docks; Joseph-Antoine Roy, *Histoire de la famille Schneider et du Creusot* (Paris, 1962), p. 160.

21. Jules Huret, *Enquête sur les grèves* (Paris, 1901), p. 15; statement by the director of the Rességuier-Carmaux glass company.

22. Pierre Bézard-Falgar, *Les Syndicats patronaux de l'industrie métallurgique en France* (Paris, 1922), pp. 99–100.

23. See Louis, *Histoire,* I, 178.

24. Even in France, resistance to high dues often had nothing to do with syndicalism or even with resistance to organization *per se.* In northern France, less than 30% of the miners were officially unionized in 1912, largely because they disliked the dues. They were definitely not syndicalist—they resisted a rival syndicalist union—and clearly felt loyal to their union whether they were in it or not. On membership fluctuations in Germany, see Deutsche Metallarbeiter-Verband, *Jahr- und Handbuch,* 1912. On hostility to union bureaucracy and the desire for local democracy see Philipp A. Koller, *Das Massen- und Führerproblem in den Freien Gewerkschaften* (Tübingen, 1930) and Alan Fox, *A History of the National Union of Boot and Shoe Operatives 1874–1957* (Oxford, 1958). A precise comparison is of course difficult. Quarrels over bureaucracy were more frequent in Germany and Britain because there was more bureaucracy. At the least, however, the issues that historians of France have considered as determined by French character and syndicalism were endemic to the union movement at this point.

25. Syndicat national des travailleurs des chemins de fer, *Compte rendu du dix-huitième Congrès national* (Paris, 1907), p. 65; Comité central des houillères de France, *Circulaire No. 3137: Syndicat des mineurs du Pas-de-Calais* (Paris, 1906), p. 4; AD Nord M626/65; Fédération française des travailleurs du livre, *Compte-rendu du neuvième congrès national* (Paris, 1905), p. 19.

26. Fédération . . . du Livre, *Compte-rendu,* p. 238.

27. *Ibid.,* p. 79.

28. AN F[7]12916, on agitation in Paris after the Villeneuve–Saint Georges incident. See also AD Bouches-du-Rhône M6-10826, on promptings of violence in Aix in 1913 by syndicalist leaders.

29. AD Loire-Atlantique 1M2319, report of 1907.

30. APS B/a 1351, report of Dec. 28, 1909.

31. AN F[7]13867, report of Dec. 28, 1909.

32. AN F[7]12917, on riots in Draveil, 1908.

33. AN F[7]12786, report of Aug. 8, 1906.

34. Fédération nationale des syndicats d'ouvriers coiffeurs, *Compte rendu des travaux du 7e congrès national* (Bourges, 1909), p. 50.

35. Archives de la Fédération nationale des travailleurs du bâtiment, statement in 1908.

36. APS B/a 1406, surveillance of the C.G.T. general strike committee, 1900–1901. Briand's book, *La Grève générale,* was published in Paris, n.d.

37. AN F[7]13269.

38. AD Bouches-du-Rhône M6-2049, report of Sept. 6, 1909.

39. AD Isère 116M/9, report of Sept. 15, 1905.

40. Arthur M. Ross and Paul Hartman, *Changing Patterns of Industrial*

Conflict (New York, 1960), p. 124. The specific discussion of syndicalism's relationship to strike rates, interesting despite its attribution of far too much importance to syndicalist guidance, is J. Juilliard's "Le Syndicalisme révolutionnaire et les grèves," *Mouvement social* (1968), pp. 55–69.

41. Raoul Briquet, "La Grève et le contrat du travail," *La Revue socialiste* (1904), p. 730; AD Nord M625/89, on the La Gorgue-Estaires strike; *L'Ouvrier textile,* Oct. 1, 1911; A. and Z., "Pour la réduction des heures du travail," *La Revue socialiste* (1906), p. 314; APS B/a 1360, on the origins of the railroad strike; Fédération nationale de la céramique, *Compte-rendu du IVe congrès national* (Bourges, 1904), p. 31; AD Vosges 98M98², report of May 1909.

42. Time and time again, particularly in Paris, strikes were voted by only a minority of those present. A meeting of Paris carpenters before the 1906 strike was attended by 1,500 of the 3,000 carpenters in the area; but only 587 of those present voted (200 of these were opposed) and only 1,000 ultimately joined the strike. In such strike meetings a minority of zealots could dominate the vote, though not necessarily the ultimate strike. Many meetings in Paris also were heavily influenced by unemployed workers, anxious to share and to voice their misery and, often, to receive strike benefits.

43. AD Loire 92M/197 (on votes forced by the syndicalist miners' union, to 1912) and 92M/168 (on forced votes by construction workers in 1910); Fédération nationale de l'industrie textile, *Compte rendu du XIe congrès national ouvrier de l'industrie textile* (Lille, 1909), p. 31. For the shocked Anglo-Saxon reaction to voting procedures, see Henry Steele, *The Working Classes in France, a Social Study* (London, 1904), pp. 53 ff.

44. AD Bouches-du-Rhône M6-3406bis, on Marseilles in 1900; AD Tarn IVM²98A, on the general strike in Mazamet.

45. Pétrus Faure, *Histoire du mouvement ouvrier dans le département de la Loire* (Saint-Étienne, 1956), p. 280; Antony Schoux, *Des Grèves maritimes* (Paris, 1910), p. 99.

46. APS B/a 1377, on printers' strikes, 1902–1906; A. and Z., "Pour la réduction," pp. 133 and 593; Hubert Lagardelle, "Chronique sociale," *Mouvement socialiste* (1901), p. 750; Fédération des ouvriers des métaux et similaires de France, *Rapport de l'exercice du 1er juillet 1909 au 21 mars 1911* (Paris, 1911), p. 25; Fédération corporative des mouleurs en métaux de France, *Compte rendu officiel du 7e congrès national* (Paris, 1908), p. 18; Union fédérale des ouvriers métallurgistes de France, Chambre syndicale des ouvriers métallurgistes et parties similaires, *Statuts* (Paris, 1902), p. 26: Fédération nationale des travailleurs de l'industrie du bâtiment, *Congrès du bâtiment* (Orléans, 1910), pp. 68, 177.

47. Léon de Seilhac, *La Grève* (Paris, 1903), pp. 194–95; VP Dec. 15, 1906; Léon de Seilhac, *Les Grèves du Tarn* (Paris, 1910), p. 93; AN F⁷12917, on Draveil, 1908.

48. APS B/a 1351 (bakers, 1903), 1369 (carpenters' strikes, 1899–1907), and 1379 (coachmen's strikes, 1901–1904), all cases of syndicalist involvement in the "fox hunt." Miners (and many other workers) of course used the same tactics without syndicalist inspiration; see reports on the 1900 strike in AD Nord M626/23.

Chapter 2

1. André Bourgeois, "Quatre jours chez les grévistes," *Pages libres* (1901), p. 184; AD Loire 92M/92, on the Saint-Étienne strike.
2. AN F⁷13267–13271, reports on May 1 demonstrations, 1906–1914; APS B/a 1628, May Day activities, 1900–1914.
3. APS B/a 1362, surveillance of political groups during the railroad strike; *Le Révolté* (du Pas-de-Calais), Dec. 22, 1912; AD Bouches-du-Rhône M6-2059, on the Dec. 16, 1912 strike.
4. APS B/a 1351; A. Luquet, "La Suppression des Bureaux de placement," *Mouvement socialiste* (1904), pp. 504, 518.
5. AD Bouches-du-Rhône M6-2047, statement by a miner in 1907.
6. AN F⁷13797, reports on pension law protests in 1910.
7. VP Sept. 20, 1908; C. Géeroms, "L'Affaire Durand," *La Vie ouvrière* (1910), p. 757; AN F⁷13568, on efforts to plan solidarity strikes in 1909–1910.
8. On British solidarity strikes right before the war, see George Dangerfield, *The Strange Death of Liberal England 1910–1914* (New York, 1951). For the whole period 1899–1914, strikes over union and solidarity issues were almost five times more important in Britain, as a percentage of all strikes, than they were in France. See Board of Trade, *Annual Reports of Strikes and Lockouts.* For the incidence and evolution of strike demands in France, see Appendix B. On Berlin-Moabit, see Helmut Bleiber, "Die Moabiter Unruhen 1910," *Zeitschrift für Geschichteswissenschaft* (1955), pp. 173–211.
9. APS B/a 1628; Charles Rist, "Chronique ouvrière," *Revue d'économie politique* (1908), p. 113; AD Loire 92M/140. The most general account is A. and Z., "Pour la réduction des heures du travail," *La Revue socialiste* (1906), pp. 129–144, 307–323, 433–451, 592–605, 718–733.
10. On agitation to cut hours of work in Germany, see Deutsche Metallarbeiter-Verband, *Jahr- und Handbuch für Verbandsmitgleider,* 1911–1913; Marie Bernays, *Untersuchungen über die Schwankungen der Arbeits-intensität während der Arbeitswoche und während der Arbeitstages* (Leipzig, 1912); Max Mayer, *Die Anregungen Taylors für den Baubetrieb* (Berlin, 1915); Walter Schmitz, "Regelung der Arbeitszeit und Intensität der Arbeit," *Thünen-Archiv* (1911), pp. 165–328. Overall, strikes for hours reduction comprised 17% of the total in Germany, compared to 15.5% in France.
11. *Congrès national des mineurs de France, tenu à Carmaux* (Saint-Étienne, 1903), p. 40; P. G. La Chesnais, "Les Grèves du Pas-de-Calais," *Pages libres* (1906), p. 356; AN F⁷13788, on miners' congresses 1900–1913.

12. Fédération nationale de la céramique, *Compte-rendu du IVᵉ congrès national* (Bourges, 1904), p. 17.

13. Gaston Grandgeorge and Louis Guérin, *L'Industrie textile en France en 1904* (Paris, 1905), pp. 51, 83 ff.; AN F²²168–69, on Flers and Graulhet in 1907.

14. *Bulletin de la Chambre syndicale des ouvriers peintres en bâtiment de la Seine*, May, 1909; AN F⁷13610, report on the Bourse du travail in Saint-Malo (1912), which includes interviews with union leaders on the difficulty of arousing construction workers for positive gains; Maurice Halbwachs, *La Classe ouvrière et les niveaux de vie* (Paris, 1913), pp. 443–45.

15. Ministère du commerce, de l'industrie, des postes et des télégraphes: office du travail, *Rapport sur l'apprentissage dans les industries de l'ameublement* (Paris, 1905), pp. 531, 647; "Trois grandes grèves," *La Revue syndicaliste* (1909), p. 51.

16. Chambre syndicale des dessinateurs de Nantes, *La Première grève des dessinateurs* (Nantes, 1907), p. 4; AD Vosges 8 M 99¹, on a 1907 strike; Raoul Briquet, "La Grève générale des mineurs," *Mouvement socialiste* (1903), p. 68; AN F²²170, on Nantes.

17. AD Meurthe-et-Moselle M/610; Léon de Seilhac, *Le Lock-out de Fougères* (Paris, 1907), p. 36; AD Gironde 1909, scattered strikes.

18. APS B/a 1369; A. G. Rouchy, *Les Grèves dans les chemins de fer* (Paris, 1912), *passim*.

19. In one Welsh mining village, the price rise was not reported to most families until 1907, five years after the inflation began; Wil Jon Edwards, *From the Valley I Came* (London, 1958), p. 46.

20. AN F²²167, strike by Annonay paper workers in 1906.

21. AD Bouches-du-Rhône M6-2059.

22. AD Seine-et-Oise M Strikes 1911–1913. See also, for statements on the inflation, AD Loire 92M/219, ditchdiggers' strikes, 1913; AN F⁷13647, carpenters' strikes, 1899–1907 (see especially the report on a Lyons strike in 1905); APS B/a 1369, activities by the building trades' unions; AD Vosges 8 M 101¹, strikes in Raon-l'Étape, 1907.

23. AN F⁷13826, on several dock strikes after 1909 which reveal the transition to positive wage demands after a reaction to technologically adjusted rates (due to new cranes); AD Bouches-du-Rhône M6-2058, metalworkers' strikes over rates on new machines, 1907; Fédération française des travailleurs du livre, *Compte-rendu du neuvième congrès national* (Paris, 1905), p. 53.

24. Léon de Seilhac, *La Grève du tissage de Lille* (Paris, 1910), p. 63.

25. AN F⁷12787, reports on construction strikes in 1908 and F²²167, reports on 1905–1906 construction strikes, particularly in Paris.

26. APS B/a 1402.

27. AD Seine-et-Oise M Strikes, 1911–1913, reports on an "awakening" of unskilled construction workers in the department after 1910, beginning with public works laborers on the newly nationalized railroads. Ministère du travail

et de la prévoyance sociale: direction du travail, *Salaires et durée du travail* (Paris, 1907), p. 297; Paul Bureau, *Le Contrat du travail* (Paris, 1902), p. 27; AD Loire 92M/122, reports on the first wave of carters' strikes in Saint-Étienne, in 1903.

28. Fritz Paeplow, *Zur Geschichte der deutschen Bauarbeiterbewegung* (Berlin, n.d.); August Bringman, "Zur Kämpfe im Baugewerbe," *Die Neue Zeit* (1909–1910), pp. 205–210; Zentralverband der Maurer u. Bauhilfsarbeiter Deutschlands, *Jahrbuch 1910* (Hamburg, 1911); *Grundstein*, 1906–1909.

29. AN F⁷13648, union statement in 1913.

30. "La Grève des mineurs de la Loire et l'arbitrage," *Musée social* (1900), p. 37.

31. AN F⁷13868.

32. APS B/a 1387; AD Pas-de-Calais M1794; Adrien Veber, "Mouvement social," *La Revue socialiste* (1900), p. 370. On the incidence of strike demands in the major industries, see Appendix B.

33. Fédération française des travailleurs du livre, *8ième Congrès national* (Paris, 1900), p. 19; AD Isère 166M/8, on leatherworkers' demands for written rates in 1904, in Grenoble; AN F⁷13867, also on leatherworkers, 1909–1911; AD Nord M625/35, on the textile strike in Halluin, which revolved around demands for a written agreement.

34. AN F⁷13872, on dockers' efforts to cut hours of work in various cities; *L'Ouvrier textile*, Dec. 1, 1911; Achille Maertens, *La Grève du tissage Plancke d'Hazebrouck* (Lille, 1908), p. 10.

35. AN F⁷13647, on Saint-Malo; includes an extremely detailed report on construction and other workers in the whole area; APS B/a 1377 and 1380, accounts of abortive campaigns for hours reduction by printers and masons, 1906–1909.

36. AN F⁷12766, reports on characteristic agitation in the glass industry, where the standard workers' arguments for hours reduction were frequently developed, and 13868, on Fougères; AD Bouches-du-Rhône M6-2043, on the 1902 strike in the merchant marine, which again provides good examples of the contrast between workers' statements on hours reductions and union literature on the subject; AD Nord M621/24, tramway workers in the Nord.

37. Ministère du travail et de la prévoyance sociale: office du travail, *Enquête sur la réduction de la durée du travail le samedi (semaine anglaise)* (Paris, 1913), p. 243.

38. The incidence of strikes over personal issues was about 25% higher in France than in other industrial countries between 1899 and 1914. Roughly 20% of the strikes in Germany concerned such issues, for example. See *Tabellen zur Statistik der Lohnbewegungen, Streiks, und Aussperrungen im Jahre 1903–1913*, in Generalkommission der deutschen Gewerkschaften, *Correspondanzblatt*, 1904–1914.

39. STAT, *passim;* see Appendix B.

40. Ministère du travail, *Enquête,* p. 245. There are many reports of strikes

over personal issues; particularly important are those dealing with metalworkers: AN F⁷13774 (agitation by merchant seamen 1909–1910); APS B/a 1387 (strikes by metalworkers, 1903–1905); AD Loire 92M/203 (strikes in metallurgy, 1909–1910); AD Bouches-du-Rhône M6-2050 (agitation among Marseilles metalworkers, 1912–1914).

41. Gabriel Beaubois, "Le Mouvement ouvrier à Limoges," *Mouvement socialiste* (1905), p. 74; AN F⁷13601 includes an extended report on the activities of the Saint-Malo Bourse du travail, 1911–13, and its embarrassed relations with French harbor construction workers who struck against imported Spanish labor; AN F⁷13648, on the building workers' federation, deals with the agitation among barracks-builders in eastern France.

42. AD Gironde 1900 Strikes (on tramway workers).

43. *L'Ouvrier textile*, Dec. 1, 1904.

44. AN F⁷13867, report of July 1911.

45. APS B/a 1399 bis, report of 1905.

46. *L'Action syndicale* (du Pas-de-Calais), Feb. 14, 1904.

47. AD Saône-et-Loire 194M/27, in a Montceau strike meeting, Oct. 21, 1911.

48. APS B/a 1359, report of Oct. 6, 1909, on a carters' strike.

49. Adrien Veber, "Mouvement social," *La Revue socialiste* (1901), pp. 361, 362, statements by individual sailors in the 1901 strikes, the first in Le Havre and the second in Marseilles.

50. AD Saône-et-Loire 194M/14, on the Le Creusot strike; *Le Réveil du Nord*, May 5, 1906; Maurice Kahn, "Les Evènements de Limoges," *Pages libres* (1905), p. 4; AD Pas-de-Calais M1803, reports on miners' strikes involving complaints against favoritism, 1903–1906.

51. Louis Maurice and A. Chaboseau, "Mouvement syndical," *La Revue socialiste* (1905), pp. 721–22.

52. Léon Laroche, *Montceau-les-Mines* (Montceau-les-Mines, 1924), pp. 129–30.

53. AN F⁷13887, on strikes in the merchant marine, 1910–1914; AD Seine-et-Oise M Strikes, 1909, on the quarry workers; APS B/a 1352, on Parisian waiters.

54. Alphonse Merrheim, "Le Mouvement ouvrier dans les bassins de Longwy," *Mouvement socialiste* (1905), pp. 447–448, statement by a worker.

55. *Ibid.*, p. 448; AD Meurthe-et-Moselle wM/ 613; AN F²²169.

56. AD Rhône, Série M, strikes, 1901, report of Jan. 31, 1901, from a union poster.

57. Antony Schoux, *Des Grèves maritimes* (Paris, 1910), p. 96; André E. Sayous, *Les Grèves de Marseilles en 1904* (Paris, 1904), p. 10; *Le Musée social: Annales* (1904), p. 475.

58. *L'Ouvrier textile*, Apr. 1, 1913; *Le Réveil du Nord*, Mar. 14, 1906; Charles Rist, "Chronique ouvrière," *Revue d'économie politique* (1905), p. 556; AN F⁷12915, on Paris subway workers in 1908.

59. AN $F^7$13923, on the Parisian coachmen, and F^{22}169, on Dôle in 1907; AD Vosges 8 M 101^1, on Raon-l'Etape in 1907. Other interesting cases are: AD Nord M625/122 and 124, on textile workers in Roubaix and Tourcoing in 1911, when woolcombers were just beginning to come to the defense of union leaders on a personal basis.

60. Léon de Seilhac, La Grève (Paris, 1903), p. 65; AD Meurthe-et-Moselle wM/ 611, on Lorraine in 1905: Léon de Seilhac, Les Grèves du Chambon (Paris, 1912), p. 26; AN $F^7$12781, on Le Creusot in 1901.

61. VP July 21, 1907; AN $F^7$13622, on efforts by the truckers' unions, and 13700, on Sète.

62. AD Meurthe-et-Moselle wM/ 612, on strikes by textile workers in 1907, where the demand for worker delegates loomed large; AD Nord M619/32, agitation by bakers in Lille, 1904; the bakers, who were not concerned with union rights or representatives, pleaded for the establishment of channels through which complaints could be communicated to their employers.

63. Charles Rist, "Chronique ouvrière," Revue d'économie politique (1904), p. 588; AD Seine-et-Oise XIV M, on willingness to bargain during the 1910 railroad strike.

64. An F^{22}169, on Mont-de-Marson; Henry Steele, The Working Classes in France, a Social Study (London, 1904), p. 78.

65. Ministère du travail et de la prévoyance sociale: office du travail, Enquête sur le travail à domicile dans l'industrie de la chaussure (Paris, 1914), p. 369.

66. De Seilhac, Grèves du Chambon, p. 38.

67. AN $F^7$13699, on Grenoble; G. Dumoulin, "Les Conventions d'Arras," La Vie ouvrière (1910), p. 690; Jules Uhry, "Les Grèves en 1901," Mouvement socialiste (1903), p. 553.

68. APS B/a 1353, reports of Dec. 1911 and Mar. 1912, on the cab-drivers, and 1358, on the jewelers; AD Isère 166M/9, on bitter strikes by Voiron silk workers; Archives de la Féderation nationale des travailleurs du bâtiment; AD Vosges 8 M 101^1, on Raon-l'Étape in 1907; Joseph-Antoine Roy, Histoire de la famille Schneider et du Creusot (Paris, 1962), p. 100; AN F^{22}167.

69. STAT, passim.

70. STAT, passim; Isidore Finance, Les Syndicats professionels devant les tribunaux et le parlement depuis 1884 (Paris, 1911), pp. 205 ff.

71. AD Nord M627/6.

72. AD Loire 92M/193, report of Dec. 1911, on Lorette; AN $F^7$12791, on Cagnac.

73. VP Aug. 5, 1906; Adrien Veber, "Mouvement social," La Revue socialiste (1904), p. 110; AN $F^7$13773, on Doincourt.

74. L'Ouvrier textile, Apr. 1, 1910.

75. Albin Huart, L'Industrie du bouton dans l'Oise et ses grèves récentes (Paris, 1910), p. 20; AN $F^7$13891, on Chambon; Léon de Seilhac, Les Grèves du Tarn (Paris, 1910), p. 93.

76. De Seilhac, *Grève du tissage*, p. 88; AN F⁷13699, on Tornay. AD Tarn IV M²98B recounts a similar incident in Graulhet in 1910.

77. *La Bataille syndicaliste*, Sept. 1, 1911; AN F²²168.

78. APS B/a 1351, on Parisian bakers in 1903, and 1419, on barbers between 1907 and 1910.

79. AN F⁷13923, on crimes during and after the railroad strike.

80. Public Records Office HO 21247.

81. AD Loire 92M/92, on Saint-Étienne; APS B/a 1351 and 1394, on the Parisian tailors; AD Nord M625/7, on Armentières.

Chapter 3

1. Fédération nationale de la céramique, *Compte-rendu du IVᵉ congrès national* (Bourges, 1904), p. 31.

2. Raoul Briquet, "La Grève et le contrat du travail," *La Revue socialiste* (1904), p. 730; *L'Ouvrier textile*, Oct. 1, 1911; A. and Z., "Pour la réduction des heures du travail," *La Revue socialiste* (1906), p. 314; APS B/a 1360, reports on agitation in 1909 by truckers, new to strike activity. On the problem of endemic spontaneous strikes in Roubaix textiles, see the reports in AD Nord M625/89.

3. AN F²²168 and 169, reports of March 1907 on Grazac. For other instances of tension between spontaneous agitation and syndicalist leadership, see A. Luquet, "La Suppression des bureaux de placement," *Mouvement socialiste* (1904), p. 504; *Le Réveil du Nord*, Mar. 13, 1906; Pierre du Marousseur, "La Vie chère et les grèves de consommateurs," *La Reforme sociale* (1911), p. 730.

4. Confédération générale du travail, *XIᵉ Congrès corporatif* (Paris, 1900), p. 106; see also Comité de propagande de la grève générale, *La Grève générale* (Paris, 1901), p. 3.

5. AN F²²168; André Bourgeois, "Quatre Jours chez les grévistes," *Pages libres* (1901), p. 178; APS B/a 1386, on C.G.T. activities in 1902; AD Nord M626/64, reports on arrests during the 1906 mine strike, which reflect the paucity of leaders the syndicalists could provide.

6. Syndicalist speeches during strikes contrast fascinatingly with those by socialists, which were far more theoretical and directed towards the future society. Unlike syndicalists, socialists refrained from converting their strictures against capitalism to vigorous attacks against individual manufacturers involved in a dispute. A revealing collection of socialist speeches made during the 1905 Ruhr mine strike, Regierung Arnsberg I #62, is in the Münster Staatsarchiv.

7. Jean Vial, *La Coutume chapelière* (Paris, 1941), p. 340; Pierre Coupat, "Les Grèves de la mécanique," *La Revue syndicaliste* (1906), p. 27.

8. Fédération nationale des travailleurs de l'industrie du bâtiment, *Compte rendu des travaux du IVᵉ congrès national* (Paris, 1912), p. 166.

9. AN F⁷12783, reports of Dec. 1906. These reports, on the northern miners'

150 REVOLUTIONARY SYNDICALISM AND FRENCH LABOR

strike, deal with the problem of fund raising and public support quite extensively; the problem was particularly acute in massive strikes of this sort.

10. APS B/a 1360, accounts of the 1910 railroad strike which discuss reasons for nonparticipation in the Paris area; they include direct statements from workers citing family size and resultant poverty or wifely opposition to the financial risk of an unaided strike as reasons they must stay on the job. See also Fédération corporative des mouleurs en métaux de France, *Compte rendu officiel du VIe congrès national* (Paris, 1906), pp. 28 ff. Lack of adequate strike aid was common in all countries; here too France's comparative distinctiveness must be qualified. Miners and the unskilled rarely received union help anywhere. Only French construction workers were deprived of regular strike aid by syndicalist leadership, for a short period.

11. Edouard Bernstein, *La Grève et le lockout en Allemagne* (Brussels, 1908), *passim.*

12. AD Ille-et-Vilaine 60 Ma/3, on the calming influence of syndicalist leaders in Fougères. For similar efforts in Paris, among truckers and machinists respectively, see APS B/a 1360 and 1384.

13. Fédération nationale de l'industrie textile, *Compte rendu du congrès national ouvrier de l'industrie textile* (Lille, 1913), *passim;* Fédération nationale du bâtiment et des travaux publics, *Congrès, 1910. Fascicule C* (Paris, 1910), *passim;* AN F⁷13773, on Merrheim in Le Chambon, and F⁷13867, on Dret's policies in leatherworkers' strikes, 1909–1911; Archives de la Fédération nationale des travailleurs du bâtiment, report of 1910.

14. Syndicat national des travailleurs des chemins de fer, *Rapport du Conseil d'administration présenté au 20e Congrès national* (Paris, 1909), p. 93.

15. A. and Z., "Pour la réduction," pp. 130, 726; Fédération française des travailleurs du livre, *Dixième congrès national* (Paris, 1910), p. 53; Camille Toureng, "La Grève de l'imprimerie (avril-mai, 1906); ses conséquences," *Pages libres* (1906), p. 309; Alfred Lambert, *Le Mouvement social en France, 1902–1904* (Paris, 1904), p. 17; Ministère du travail et de la prévoyance sociale: direction du travail, *Rapports sur l'application des lois réglementant le travail en 1912* (Paris, 1914), p. cxxi.

16. STAT, *passim;* for this and subsequent points, see Appendix B.

17. STAT, *passim.*

18. APS B/a 1403, on new police tactics affecting the Parisian building trades; Leo A. Loubère, "Left-Wing Radicals, Strikes, and the Military, 1880–1907," *French Historical Studies* (Spring, 1963).

19. AN F⁷12773, for the 1913 directive and for the decline in the number of troops to be sent to major strikes; AD Ille-et-Vilaine 60 Mb/8, on Fougères.

20. STAT, *passim.*

21. Compagnie générale transatlantique, *Assemblée générale des actionnaires du 29 juin 1901* (Paris, 1901), p. 14; Compagnie générale transatlantique, *Assemblée générale des actionnaires du 31 mai 1910* (Paris, 1910), p. 18. For more extended treatment of employers' policies see Peter N. Stearns, "Against

the Strike Threat; Employer Policy toward Labor Agitation in France, 1900–1914," *Journal of Modern History* (1968), pp. 474–500.

22. André E. Sayous, *Les Grèves de Marseilles en 1904* (Paris, 1910), p. 47.

23. Vial, *Coutume*, p. 274; Jacques Expert-Bezançon, *Les Organisations de défense patronale* (Paris, 1911), p. 110; AN $F^{22}167$, on preliminary efforts by Parisian masonry contractors, 1906–1908; Charles Rist, "Chronique ouvrière," *Revue d'économie politique* (1908), p. 533.

24. Archives de la Fédération nationale des travailleurs du bâtiment, report of 1910; AD Bouches-du-Rhône M6-2040, on the 1904 lockout in Marseilles; Sayous, *Grèves*, p. 54.

25. APS B/a 1368, on Parisian masons after 1909; AD Bouches-du-Rhône M6-10824, on Marseilles.

26. Joseph-Antoine Roy, *Histoire de la famille Schneider et du Creusot* (Paris, 1962), p. 99; Fédération patronale et ouvrière du camionnage de Marseilles, *Statuts* (Marseilles, 1905), p. 7. On the relaxation of tensions in Montceau after 1901 through continuing conciliation, see AN $F^{7}12782$.

27. *Le Musée social: Annales* (1912), p. 361; AD Loire 92M/177, on Le Chambon.

28. STAT, *passim*.

29. STAT, *passim*.

30. AD Bouches-du-Rhône M6-10827, on Marseilles in 1912.

31. Léon de Seilhac, *La Grève des cheminots* (Paris, 1911), p. 402.

32. APS B/a 1360, statement by Lévèque, secretary of the Paris food workers' union, Apr. 29, 1909.

33. AN $F^{7}13868$, on Fougères.

34. AN $F^{7}13699$, on Saint-Étienne in 1912 and before.

35. AN $F^{7}13868$, on Fougères; APS B/a 1370 deals with diversions provided for Parisian coachmen; AD Nord M621/31, on printers' procedures during strikes.

36. On changes in picketing and aid distribution procedures in Paris, APS B/a 1352 and 1356 (bakers), 1358 (jewelers), 1360 (truckers), 1373 (electricians; the reports show an unusually direct contrast between strikes in 1903 and in 1910), 1379 (masons in 1909), and 1401 (ditchdiggers, 1907–1908); AN $F^{7}13868$, on Fougères.

37. APS B/a 1627, reports of 1911, 1912, and 1913, on May Day activities; AD Bouches-du-Rhône M6-10825 provides another account of declining violence, among cabinetmakers in Marseilles. On Lille, AD Nord M625/32.

38. AD Ille-et-Vilaine 60 Ma/3, on Fougères.

39. AN $F^{7}12784$, on rising interest in negotiations among Parisian masons in 1905; *L'Action syndicale* (du Pas-de-Calais), Aug. 30, 1908; STAT, *passim*.

40. Fédération nationale des syndicats ouvriers du bâtiment, *2ème Congrès* (Puteaux, 1904), p. 17; AD Bouches-du-Rhône M6-10826, on merchant seamen's agitation for legislation.

41. J. Lapierre, "Les Grèves des platrières du bassin de Paris," *La Vie*

ouvrière (1912), p. 115; Charles Gide and others, *Le Droit de grève* (Paris, 1909), p. 221. See APS B/a 1373, on contracts for Parisian electricians.

42. *L'Ouvrier textile,* Apr. 1, 1910, Apr. 1 and June 1, 1913; Confédération générale du travail, *XVIIe Congrès corporatif* (Paris, 1911), pp. 303–304; Georges Airelle, "Les Grèves de la Haute Meurthe," *Pages libres* (1905), p. 611; Maurice Petitcollot, *Les Syndicats textiles dans l'arrondissement de Lille* (Lille, n.d.), p. 313; AN F^{22}167.

43. Confédération générale du travail, *XVIIe Congrès,* p. 305.

44. Charles Rist, "Chronique ouvrière," *Revue d'économie politique* (1908), p. 114; Gide, *Droit,* p. 221; Raymond Joran, *L'Organisation syndicale dans l'industrie des bâtiments* (Paris, 1914), pp. 173–175, 180 ff.; AN F^{7}13619 and 13847; *Tarif des prix de main-d'oeuvre de la menuiserie de la ville de Cholet* (Cholet, 1907), *passim;* AD Rhône, strikes, 1910.

45. AD Seine-Maritime, Commerce et industrie, strikes in the latter half of 1910: Report on the settlement of a cabinetmakers' strike in Rouen:

Collective work contract drawn up after the conciliation procedures directly established between the cabinetmakers of Rouen and its environs on strike and the employers in this craft, who have declared that the strike which broke out November 4 had ended amiably on the conditions here listed:

Article I. All cabinetmakers and machinists will receive a 5-centime-per-hour raise. The normal rate and the minimum for hourly wages is set at .60 francs.

Article II. The hours of work will be paid in the following manner: for the first twelve hours, the regular rate; from the twelfth to the fourteenth, time and a half; after the fourteenth, double pay. For Sunday work, when the worker works only until 11 A.M. or noon, an extra hour will be paid; and for afternoon work, he will be paid time and a half. The hour and a half for lunch will be maintained for the summer; to be reduced to an hour in winter, agreement between employers and workers will be necessary.

Article III. During night work, paid at the rate indicated in article II, a meal will be provided by the employer or will be paid for at the rate of 1.50 francs per worker. The time for this meal, which will not exceed an hour, will not be paid for.

Article IV. Wages will be paid in the shops as is customary for each company. And in shops and companies where pay is given every two weeks, an advance of 30 francs will be given the Saturday between paydays, on request. The employers in general pledge morally and insofar as it is possible to use a system of pay, either by their foremen or in some other manner, that will permit payment to be completed by the end of the workday.

Article V. As to the methods of hiring and firing, no change will be made in the usages and customs of the craft. However, any employer who fires a worker for insufficient work should warn him an hour before the end of the day. Any worker who quits voluntarily or is dismissed by the employer will be paid immediately and should take his tools away, and the employer is not responsible and cannot be sued for disappearance, loss, or theft of tools or wood.

Article VI. A bonus of .50 francs per fortnight will be paid to each worker for supplying and maintaining his tools.

Article VII. For every job between one and five kilometers outside town, the travel expenses will be paid, plus an hour's extra wages.

Article VIII. For every job requiring the worker to stay overnight, 2.50 francs per day extra will be paid, Sundays and holidays and losses of time included; however, when the worker cannot work at least a half day on Sundays and holidays, the displacement fee will be three francs. Each worker will be given a paid trip every four weeks, up to a distance of 30 kilometers; beyond this, an agreement will be made between employer and worker.

Article IX. No worker will be dismissed for wishing to limit his work day to 11 hours, or for the strike. The employers pledge not to put any worker on the index.

Article X. The present collective agreement is valid for three years, beginning Jan. 1, 1911, with retroactive effect from Nov. 8, 1910, the day when work was resumed. The contract will be renewed for new periods of three years. It can be denounced by either party three months before its expiration. The present contract has been drawn up before the Justice of the Peace of the 3rd canton.

46. AN F⁷13867 and 13881; P. Cousteix, "Le Mouvement ouvrier limousin de 1870 à 1939," *L'Actualité de l'histoire* (Dec. 1957), p. 74; Charles Rist, "Chronique ouvrière," *Revue d'économie politique* (1907), p. 130.

47. AD Pas-de-Calais M1790; *Convention fixant les conditions du travail des ouvriers de ports, docks et môles dans les ports de Marseilles* (Marseilles, 1903), *passim;* Rist, "Chronique" (1908), p. 115; AD F⁷13619.

48. AD Nord M621/31; A. and Z., "Pour la réduction," p. 131; Fédération . . . du livre, *Dixième congrès*, p. 53.

49. G. Dumoulin, "Les Conventions d'Arras," *La Vie ouvrière* (1910), p. 682; Raoul Briquet, "La Grève générale des mineurs," *Mouvement socialiste* (1903), p. 187; AN F⁷12791.

50. AN F⁷13788, on the Loire miners; *L'Ouvrier textile,* June 1, 1913; Comité des Houillères de la Loire, *Convention signée le 22 juillet 1910* (Saint-Étienne, 1911), pp. 3, 10; Rist, "Chronique" (1908), p. 115.

51. *L'Ouvrier textile,* June 1, 1913.

52. "La Grève des mineurs de la Loire et l'arbitrage," *Musée social,* (1900), p. 51; Léon de Seilhac, *La Grève du tissage de Lille* (Paris, 1910), p. 28; AN F⁷13820 (on Armentières) and 13869 (on the Mazamet leatherworkers); AD Nord M625/12, on Armentières; Fédération française des travailleurs du livre, *Compte rendu du neuvième congrès national* (Paris, 1905), p. 128.

53. Compagnie du chemin de fer de Paris à Orléans. *Assemblée générale des actionnaires du 29 mars 1912* (Paris, 1912), p. 41.

54. P. Pic, "Les Enseignements de quelques grèves récentes," *Revue d'économie politique* (1912), p. 14; A. Picart, "La Grève de la maçonnerie parisienne," *Mouvement socialiste* (1909), pp. 381 ff.; AN F⁷13693; Léon Jouhaux, "Le Syndicalisme révolutionnaire chez les travailleurs de l'état," *La Vie ouvrière* (1910), p. 477.

55. Fédération . . . du livre, *Compte rendu*, p. 128.

56. Fédération des métaux, *Compte rendu du deuxième congrès* (Paris, 1913), p. 108.

57. Paul Louis, *Histoire du socialisme en France* (Paris, 1950), p. 289.

58. Édouard Dolléans, *Alphonse Merrheim* (Paris, n.d.), p. 23.

59. Alphonse Merrheim, "La Grève d'Hennebont," *Mouvement socialiste* (1906), p. 203.

60. AD Saône-et-Loire 194M/2; P. G., "Le Mouvement ouvrier dans la région vosgienne," *Pages libres* (1905), p. 93; Alphonse Merrheim, "Le Mouvement ouvrier dans les bassins de Longwy," *Mouvement socialiste* (1905), p. 426; Michelle Perrot, "Aperçus sur le mouvement ouvrier et socialiste dans le Calvados (1871–1914)," *Actes du 81ᵉ congrès des sociétés savantes* (Paris, 1956), p. 766; Georges Hottenger, *Le Pays de Briey* (Paris, 1912), pp. 101, 239; Serge Bonnet, Charles Santini, and Hubert Barthélemy, "Les Italiens dans l'arrondissement de Briey avant 1914," *Annales de l'Est* (1962), pp. 31–56.

61. Leo A. Loubère, "Coal Miners, Labor Relations, and Politics in the Lower Languedoc, 1880–1914," *Journal of Social History* (1968), *passim*.

62. The meaning of socialism in the views of constituents has rarely been given serious attention. For a good start, see Claude Willard, *Le Mouvement socialiste en France (1893–1905). Les Guesdistes* (Paris, 1965).

63. For postwar developments, see Robert Wohl, *French Communism in the Making* (Stanford, 1966); Annie Kriegel, *Aux Origines du communisme français, 1914–1920* (2 vols., Paris, 1964); Annie Kriegel, *La Croissance de la CGT, 1918–1921* (Paris, 1966); Robert Goetz-Girey, *Le Mouvement des grèves en France, 1919–1962* (Paris, 1965).

64. Many observers noted that French workers read little and had scant knowledge of politics. See Paul de Rousiers, *The Labour Question in Britain*, tr. F. Herbertson (London, 1898), *passim*.

Chapter 4

1. Louis Rivière, "Les Grèves et la défense patronale," *La Réforme sociale* (1909), p. 727, speech by Louis Guérin in 1909.

2. Leo A. Loubère, "Left-Wing Radicals, Strikes, and the Military, 1880–1907," *French Historical Studies* (1963), *passim*.

3. Kerry Davidson, "The French Socialist Party and Parliamentary Efforts

to Achieve Social Reform, 1906–1914" (Ph.D. dissertation, Tulane University, 1970).

4. The theme of radical strike threat and frightened reaction can be easily followed in George Dangerfield, *The Strange Death of Liberal England, 1910–1914* (New York, 1961). A far more precise analysis is E. H. Phelps Brown, *The Growth of British Industrial Relations* (London, 1959), but even here the contrast with French workers' moderation is vivid.

5. See Eduardo Comín Colomer, *Historia del anarquismo español* (Barcelona, 1956) and Casimiro Martí, *Orígenes del anarquismo en Barcelona* (Barcelona, 1959).

6. Arthur M. Ross and Paul Hartman, *Changing Patterns of Industrial Conflict* (New York, 1960), pp. 115–140, 172–181, erroneously associates French and Italian strike patterns.

7. G. Ridker, "Discontent and Economic Growth," *Economic Development and Cultural Change* (1962–1963), pp. 1–13, presents well the common sort of expectations thesis. He correctly stresses that aspirations as well as objective economic conditions must be considered in explaining protest. But like so many students of currently "backward" areas, he implies greater and more steadily increasing expectations in the Western world than really existed during most of the industrialization process. Mancur Olson, "Rapid Growth as a Destabilizing Force," *Journal of Economic History* (1963), pp. 529–52, presents a more acceptable thesis for developing areas generally. But as such it applies to situations of growth accompanied by changes in the structure or guiding principles of the economy—not to rapid development within essentially the same structure, as in France at the turn of the century. Ted Gurr, *The Condition of Civil Violence: First Tests of a Causal Model* (Center of International Studies, Princeton University, *Research Monograph* No. 28) (Princeton, 1967) suggests hypotheses so general that they cannot be faulted but also cannot easily be applied. He finds no correlations between economic development and levels of violence and suggests a variety of factors that can be applied to France in the early twentieth century, ranging from long experience with high rates of police deterrence to the surprisingly effective performance of trade unions as outlets for a calm presentation of grievances. But we still lack a model for stages of protest once industrialization is well underway. Suggestions by George Rudé [*The Crowd in History* (New York, 1964)] and E. J. Hobsbawm [*Primitive Rebels* (New York, 1965)] about modern as contrasted with pre- or early industrial protest imply too sweeping and sudden a change. So does the fleshier but still easily grasped typology sketched in Charles Tilly, "Collective Violence in European Perspective," in Hugh Davis Graham and Ted Gurr (eds.), *Violence in America: Historical and Comparative Perspectives* (Washington, 1969), pp. 7 ff.

8. *Statistik des Deutschen Reichs,* vol. 413, Part I. In 1907, 54% of all German manufacturing workers were in companies with under fifty workers.

9. "System Ca-canny in der deutschen Schuhwareindustrie," *Zeitschrift für Sozialwissenschaft* (1909), p. 535; R. M. R. Dehn, *The German Cotton Industry* (Manchester, 1913), *passim*.

10. Georg Neuhaus, *Die deutsche Volkswirtschaft und ihre Wandlungen im letzen Vierteljahrhundert* (Berlin, 1913), II, *passim;* Jean Lescure, "Chronique des questions ouvrières," *Revue d'économie politique* (1912), p. 97; Ministère du travail et de la prévoyance sociale, *Résultats statistiques du recensement général de la population effectué le 4 mars 1906* (Paris, 1909), pp. 132, 133, 147 ff.

11. Ministère du travail, *Résultats*, pp. 147 ff.

12. Martin Wolfe, "French Interwar Stagnation Revisited," in Charles K. Warner, ed., *From the Ancien Régime to the Popular Front* (New York, 1969), p. 180 and *passim*, sketches a more balanced approach to the general question of French industrial performance than is common in the American literature.

13. This is common currency among most American students of this subject. A recent example is Reina Uirtanen, "French National Character in the Twentieth Century," in "National Character in the Perspective of the Social Sciences," *Annals of the American Academy of Political and Social Science* (1967), p. 82.

14. British workers' strike demands at the turn of the century implied many more basic grievances against the industrial structure than was the case in France and played a role in industrial retardation. A. L. Levine, *Industrial Retardation in Britain* (London, 1967). My analysis must leave open the queston of what French workers' reaction would have been if technological change had been pressed still harder. I can find no evidence that workers' protest contributed to a distinctive technological lag in the two decades before World War I; my impression is that they would have gone along with more than was imposed.

Appendix A

1. Albert Aftalion, "Le Salaire réel et sa nouvelle orientation," *Revue d'économie politique* (1912), pp. 546 ff.

2. Jean Lhomme, "Le Pouvoir d'achat de l'ouvrier français au cours d'un siècle; 1840–1940," *Mouvement social* (1968), pp. 41–69.

3. Maurice Halbwachs, "Revenus et dépenses de ménages des travailleurs. Une enquête officielle d'avant-guerre," *Revue d'économie politique* (Jan.–Feb., 1921), pp. 55–57; M. L. Dugé de Bernonville, "Enquête sur les conditions de la vie ouvrière et rurale en France en 1913–14," *Bulletin de la statistique générale de la France* (1911), p. 73 and (1913), pp. 263 ff. and (1917), pp. 190 and 198; Board of Trade (Great Britain), *Report on an Enquiry into Working Class Rents, Houses and Retail Prices . . . in the Principal Industrial Towns of France* (London, 1909).

4. See Arthur L. Bowley, *Wages and Income in the United Kingdom since 1860* (Cambridge, 1937).

5. *Bulletin de la statistique générale de la France* (1913), p. 359; Ministère *du travail et de la prévoyance sociale, Salaires et coût de l'existence à diverses époques, jusqu'en 1910* (Paris, 1911), p. 22; Ministère du commerce, de l'industrie, des postes et des télégraphes: office du travail, *Bordereaux des salaires pour diverses catégories d'ouvriers en 1900 et 1901* (Paris, 1902), p. x.

6. François Simiand, *Le Salaire, l'évolution sociale, et la monnaie* (Paris, 1932), III, Table I; Fédération nationale des travailleurs de l'industrie du bâtiment, *Annuaire* (Paris, 1911), pp. 184 ff.

7. Ministère du travail, *Salaires*, p. 22.

8. *Ibid.*

9. *Bulletin de la statistique générale de la France* (1913), *passim.*

10. *Ibid.;* Dugé de Bernonville, "Enquête," *passim;* Halbwachs, "Revenus," pp. 55–57.

11. *Bulletin de la statistique générale de la France* (1913), *passim;* Dugé de Bernonville, "Enquête," *passim.*

12. Halbwachs, "Revenus," *passim;* Maurice Halbwachs, *L'Évolution des besoins* (Paris, 1933), pp. 113–25.

13. Halbwachs, *Évolution*, p. 125; Halbwachs, "Revenus," pp. 55–56.

14. Halbwachs, "Revenus," p. 52.

15. For a concise statement of this approach, see Michelle Perrot, "Grèves, grévistes et conjoncture. Vieux problème, travaux neufs," *Mouvement social* (1968), pp. 109–24.

Bibliography

What follows is intended to suggest the main types of primary sources utilized in this study and to offer suggestions for further reading in leading secondary works.

I. Statistical material

Most important here is: Direction du travail, *Statistique des grèves et recours à conciliation*, 1899–1914 (15 vols., Paris, 1900–1915). See also the censuses of 1901, 1906, and 1911 (*Résultats statistiques du recensement général de la population*), published, in the first instance, by the Ministère du commerce, then by the Ministère du travail. For general statistical summaries, see the *Bulletin de l'Office du travail*, 1900–1914. For wages and prices, see Ministère du travail et de la prévoyance sociale, *Salaires et coût de l'existence à diverses époques, jusqu'en 1910* (Paris, 1911).

II. Archival material

The Archives nationales has many reports on major and minor strikes, on the activities of various unions, and on government plans in strike situations. Many pamphlets and union newspapers are included in some of the dossiers. The F^7 series consists of police materials, but these can cover a broad range of subjects. F^{22} has holdings from the ministries of commerce and labor, but these are not very useful and are incomplete; presumably, substantial records from these ministries remain to be opened.

The records of the Prefecture of Police in the Seine Department are invaluable and well catalogued. Departmental archives in the Series M contain police materials primarily, with press clippings often included. The quality and comprehensiveness of the records vary from department to department. Holdings in the Nord, Loire, and Bouches-du-Rhône are most elaborate, but nowhere is the coverage as complete as in Paris.

Many company records are available and somewhat useful, particularly those held in the AQ series of the Archives nationales and by the nationalized administration of mines in Saint-Étienne. Unpublished union archives are almost nonexistent in France; unions either did not keep records or lost or destroyed them subsequently.

III. Employer publications

A number of groups published useful reports on strikes, employer policies, and labor conditions. See particularly the circulars of the Comité central des houillères de France and the pamphlets by the Union des syndicats patronaux des industries textiles de la France.

IV. Union congresses and pamphlets

Reports and special publications by the C.G.T. are obviously important; each C.G.T. congress produced a complete record of deliberations. Many individual federations issued reports on congresses that are difficult but not impossible to assemble; the Musée social in Paris has the most complete and accessible holdings. Particularly useful are the publications of the Fédération des travailleurs des cuirs et peaux et similaires; the Fédération française des travailleurs du livre; the Fédération nationale de l'industrie des mines, minières et carrières de France; the Fédération nationale de l'industrie textile; the Fédération nationale des syndicats maritimes; the Fédération nationale des travailleurs de l'industrie du bâtiment; the Syndicat national des travailleurs des chemins de fer; and the Union fédérale des ouvriers métallurgistes de France.

Several union newspapers are invaluable for a study of French labor history and agitation. See: *La Bataille syndicaliste*, 1911–1914; *Le Docker*, 1907–1910; *L'Ouvrier textile*, 1904–1914; *Le Travailleur du bâtiment*, 1907–1913; *La Typographie française*, 1900–1914; *L'Union des métaux*, 1911–1914. The C.G.T. weekly, *La Voix du peuple* (1900–1914) is particularly useful.

V. Works by union and syndicalist leaders

Victor Griffuelhes, *Les Charactères du syndicalisme français* (Paris, 1908) and *Voyage révolutionnaire* (Paris, n.d.); Léon Jouhaux, *Le Syndicalisme et la C.G.T.* (Paris, 1920); E. Pataud and E. Pouget, *Comment nous ferons la révolution* (Paris, 1909); Fernand Pelloutier, *Histoire des Bourses du travail* (Paris, 1902); Émile Pouget, *L'Action directe* (Paris, n.d.) and *Le Sabotage* (Paris, n.d.); Georges Yvetot, *ABC syndicaliste* (Paris, 1908) and *Vers la grève générale* (Paris, 1901).

Special mention must of course be made of the work of Georges Sorel, the leading theorist of syndicalism, particularly of the *Réflexions sur la violence* (Paris, 1910) (translated as *Reflections on Violence*, New York, 1916).

See also, throughout the period 1900–1914, articles by union leaders on union issues, syndicalism, and specific strikes, in *La Vie ouvrière, La Revue syndicaliste, Pages libres,* and *Mouvement socialiste.*

VI. Contemporary accounts of strikes and strike movements

In addition to the many useful articles by union leaders (the most important are those by Alphonse Merrheim, in *La Vie ouvrière*) in the four periodicals listed in the previous section, see: A. and Z., "Pour la réduction des heures du travail," *La Revue socialiste* (1906), pp. 129–144; 307–323; 433–451; 592–605; 718–733 (this is the best account of the 1906 eight-hour-day movement); Aristide Briand, *Cluses!* (Paris, 1905); Yves Guyot, *La Grève des électriciens* (Paris, 1907) and *Les Chemins de fer et la grève* (Paris, 1911). A. G. Rouchy, *Les Grèves dans les chemins de fer* (Paris, 1912); André E. Sayous, *Les Grèves de Marseilles en 1904* (Paris, 1904). Antony Schoux, *Des Grèves maritimes* (Paris, 1910).

For penetrating interpretations of the strike movement generally, see Charles Rist, "Chronique ouvrière," *Revue d'économie politique,* 1904–1908 (continued by Jean Lescure, 1911–1914).

Finally, the works of Léon de Seilhac deserve special mention, including articles in the *Musée social,* but also many books; the point of view is conservative and antisyndicalist, but the factual detail is unmatched: see *La Grève du tissage de Lille* (Paris, 1910); *Le Lock-out de Fougères* (Paris, 1907); *Les Grèves du Chambon* (Paris, 1912); and *Les Grèves du Tarn* (Paris, 1910).

VII. Labor law and collective bargaining

Albert Aftalion, *La Conciliation dans les contrats collectifs* (Paris, 1911) and (with Arquembourg and Fagnot) *Le Règlement aimable des conflits du travail* (Paris, 1911); Jean-Pierre Bouère, *Le Droit de grève* (Paris, 1958) (the best historical survey); Paul Bureau, *Le Contrat de travail* (Paris, 1902) (includes much on actual strikes); Charles Gide and others, *Le Droit de grève* (Paris, 1909); Jules Huret, *Enquête sur les grèves* (Paris, 1901) (includes many interviews with employers); Léon de Seilhac, *Les Unions mixtes des patrons et ouvriers* (Paris, 1908).

VIII. On Syndicalism

Two of the best studies on syndicalism, both stressing French syndicalism, happen to be in English: J. A. Estey, *Revolutionary Syndicalism* (London, 1913), and Louis Levine, *The Labor Movement in France* (New York, 1912).

For general bibliography, see Robert Brécy, *Le Mouvement syndical en France, 1871–1921: essai bibliographique* (Paris, 1963). Two useful biographies are Édouard Dolléans, *Alphonse Merrheim* (Paris, n.d.) and Jean Maitron, *Le Syndicalisme révolutionnaire: Paul Delesalle* (Paris, 1952). For syndicalist theory see Robert Goetz-Girey, *La Pensée syndicale française* (Paris, 1948). For the background of syndicalism, see Jean Maitron, *Histoire du mouvement anarchiste en France (1880–1914)* (Paris, 1951) and André May, *Les Origines du syndicalisme révolutionnaire* (Paris, 1913). A number of contemporary articles deal with the "crisis" of syndicalism after 1910; see, for example, Paul Louis, "Y-a-t-il une crise du syndicalisme?" *La Grande Revue* (1912), 785–801; Paul Louis, *Le Syndicalisme français d'Amiens à Saint-Étienne (1900–1922)* (Paris, 1924), is also useful on this subject. On a major aspect of syndicalism, see Elisabeth Georgi, *Theorie und Praxis des Generalstreiks* (Breslau, 1908).

IX. French Labor History

Books in this section obviously relate to those listed immediately above, but they focus on union or socialist history rather than syndicalism alone.

For general French labor history, see, in English, Val R. Lorwin, *The French Labor Movement* (Cambridge, Mass., 1954). In French, Paul Louis, *Histoire du mouvement syndical en France* (2 vols., Paris, 1947) is the most convenient summary. See also Édouard Dolléans and Gérard Dehove, *Histoire du travail en France* (vol. I, Paris, 1953) and Georges Lefranc, *Histoire du mouvement syndical français* (Paris, 1937).

Far too little is available on individual unions. See Guy Chaumeil, *Histoire des cheminots et de leurs syndicats* (Paris, 1948); Henri Facdouel, *La Fédération française des travailleurs du livre* (Lyons, 1904); Max Ferré, *Histoire du mouvement syndicaliste révolutionnaire chez les instituteurs* (Paris, 1955); Raymond Joran, *L'Organisation syndicale dans l'industrie des bâtiments* (Paris, 1914); Auguste Pawlowski, *Les Syndicats jaunes* (Paris, 1911); and Jean Vial, *La Coutume chapelière* (Paris, 1941).

Two regional studies are important: Pétrus Faure, *Histoire du mouvement ouvrier dans le département de la Loire* (Saint-Étienne, 1956) and Guy Pellissier and Paul Masson, *Le Mouvement social* (vol. X of *Les Bouches-du-Rhône, encyclopédie départementale*, Paul Masson, ed., Paris, 1923).

On socialism, the outstanding work is Claude Willard, *Le Mouvement socialiste en France (1893–1905). Les Guesdistes* (Paris, 1965). Finally, though it defies precise categorization, in dealing with ideas, organizations, and strikes, see Maxime Leroy, *La Coutume ouvrière* (2 vols., Paris, 1913).

X. Working Conditions and the Working Class

Few books attempt to deal with more than a single aspect of working-class life or with a single group of workers. The most general surveys concentrate largely on wages: Michel Collinet, *L'Ouvrier français; essai sur la condition ouvrière (1900–1950)* (Paris, 1951); Jürgen Kuczynski, *Die Geschichte der Lage der Arbeiter in Frankreich von 1600 bis in die Gegenwart* (Berlin, 1949); François Simiand, *Le Salaire, l'évolution sociale, et la monnaie* (3 vols., Paris, 1932). On the related subject of prices, see Jean Lescure, *Hausses et baisses des prix de longue durée* (Paris, 1933) and Jeanne Singer-Kérel, *Le Coût de la vie à Paris de 1840 à 1954* (Paris, 1961). On the patterns of worker expenditure, two books by Maurice Halbwachs are invaluable: *La Classe ouvrière et le niveau de vie* (Paris, 1913) and *L'Évolution des besoins* (Paris, 1933).

On another level entirely, two studies of individual workers, done in the tradition of Le Play, are very helpful: Clément-Eugène Louis, *Cantonnier-poseur de voie du chemin de fer du Nord* (Paris, 1904) and M. L. de Maillard, *Décoreuse de porcelaine de Limoges* (Paris, 1903). There are useful portraits also, from a more radical vantage point, in Léon and Maurice Bonneff, *La Vie tragique des travailleurs* (Paris, 1913). Three local studies are good: Gabriel Clerc, *Passementiers stéphanois en 1912* (Saint-Étienne, 1912); Paul Bureau, *Montceau-les-Mines et le paternalisme* (La Chapelle-Montligeon, 1902); François Simon, *Petite Histoire des tisserands dans la région de Cholet* (Angers, n.d.).

Georges Mauco, *Les Étrangers en France* (Paris, 1932), gives important background. For domestic manufacturing workers, rural and urban, the most intensely studied group at the time, see the three *Enquêtes sur le travail à domicile*, by the Ministère du travail et de la prévoyance sociale: Office du travail, published between 1913 and 1917. Finally, an interesting insight into French worker and union life is given by Henry Steele, a British worker, in *The Working Classes in France, a Social Study* (London, 1904).

XI. Economic Conditions

There are a number of useful surveys of French economic history, but surprisingly few that deal adequately with the early twentieth century, despite the importance of this dynamic period in French economic development. J. H. Clapham, *The Economic Development of France and Germany, 1815–1914* (Cambridge, 1961) is still useful. For somewhat more specialized surveys, see Jean Bouvier, François Furet, and Marcel Gillet, *Le Mouvement du profit en France au XIXe siècle* (Paris, 1965) and Jean Marczewski, *Introduction à l'histoire quantitative* (Geneva, 1965). Very stimulating, though in no sense a survey, is Charles P. Kindleberger, *Economic Growth in France and Britain, 1851–1950* (Cambridge, Mass., 1954).

To supplement the general treatments, a number of local studies are useful, often treating labor conditions as well as economic activities: Marthe Barbance, *Saint-Nazaire* (Moulins, 1948); Pierre Barral, *Le Département de l'Isère sous la troisième république* (Paris, 1962); Georges Hottenger, *Le Pays de Briey* (Paris, 1912); Maxime Perrin, *La Région industrielle de Saint-Étienne* (Tours, 1939).

Among the more useful industrial studies are: Paul Baud, *Industrie chimique en France* (Paris, 1932); Pierre Clerget, *Les Industries de la soie en France* (Paris, 1925); Charles Dechelette, *L'Industrie cotonnière à Roanne* (Roanne, 1910); R. B. Forrester, *The Cotton Industry in France* (Manchester, 1921); annual reports on *L'Industrie textile en France, 1903–1907*, by Gaston Grandgeorge and Louis Guérin; L. J. Gras, *Histoire économique de la métallurgie de la Loire* (Saint-Étienne, 1908) and *Histoire économique générale des mines de la Loire* (vol. II, Saint-Étienne, 1922); Auguste Pawlowski, *La Marine marchande et l'inscription maritime* (Paris, 1910); and Joseph-Antoine Roy, *Histoire de la famille Schneider et du Creusot* (Paris, 1962).

XII. General Materials

For a primarily political narrative, see Jacques Chastenet, *Histoire de la troisième république* (vols. III and IV, Paris, 1955–1957). Pierre Laroque, *Les Rapports entre patrons et ouvriers* (Paris, 1938) offers a general historical survey of French industrial relations, to my mind quite unsatisfactory.

Six studies of strike phenomena give a vital conceptual background to the present study: R. Goetz-Girey, *Le Mouvement des grèves en France, 1919–1962* (Paris, 1965); Robert Gubbels, *La Grève, phénomène de civilisation* (Brussels, 1962); E. T. Hiller, *The Strike* (Chicago, 1928); Clark Kerr and Abraham Siegel, "The Interindustry Propensity to Strike—an International Comparison," in *Patterns of Industrial Conflict*, A. Kornhaus, R. Dubin, and A. M. Ross, eds. (New York, 1954); K. G. J. C. Knowles, *Strikes—A Study in Industrial Conflict* (Oxford, 1948); Arthur M. Ross and Paul Hartman, *Changing Patterns of Industrial Conflict* (New York, 1960).

Index

About the Author

Dr. Stearns was born in London in 1936. He took his bachelor's, master's, and doctor's degrees from Harvard University. In 1968, after teaching for five years at the University of Chicago, he accepted a professorship in history at Rutgers University and is currently Chairman of its New Brunswick Department of History. In addition to having published five books, he is Managing Editor of the *Journal of Social History* and a regular contributor to the *American Historical Review* and the *Journal of Modern History*.

The text of this book was set in Caledonia Lino-type and printed by offset on Warren's #66 Antique manufactured by S. D. Warren Company, Boston, Mass. Composed, printed and bound by Quinn & Boden Company, Inc., Rahway, N. J.